MW01519371

# Great Breeders and Their Methods

## The Hancocks

by Frank Mitchell

The Russell Meerdink Company, Ltd.
Neenah, Wisconsin 54956 U.S.A.

Cover design & layout by Bosetti Production Art & Design

Library of Congress Cataloging-in-Publication Data
Mitchell, Frank J., 1959-
    Great breeders and their methods : the Hancocks / by Frank Mitchell.
        p. cm.
    ISBN-13: 978-0-929346-78-6 (hardcover)
    1. Race horses--Breeding--Virginia--History. 2. Horse breeders--Virginia--History. 3. Hancock family. I. Title.
    SF290.U6M65 2005
    636.1'220922769423--dc22
                                        2005029561

Published by

# The Russell Meerdink Company, Ltd.

1555 South Park Avenue, Neenah, Wisconsin  54956
USA
(920) 725-0955
www.horseinfo.com

Printed in the United States of America

# TABLE OF CONTENTS

# PROLOGUE

For nearly a century and a half, the Hancock family history has run parallel to that of Thoroughbred racing in America. Over that time, changes in the economy, demographics, and social custom resonated through the sport and created the need for a careful evolution in the Hancock family's approach to raising Thoroughbreds over the past 150 years.

Under the plantation system that was the dominant economic model in the U.S. economy until the Southern conflict of 1861-65, race-horses were typically bred and raced by a few very wealthy landowners. The highly publicized North-South matches of racehorses at four-mile heats during the 1850s mirrored the growing polarization of the country over differing modes of life and politics.

After the war and due to a variety of social and economic pressures, the wealth necessary to support a string of racehorses was almost entirely vested in the wealthy sportsmen of the Northern states. These new urban owners inflated the demand for racing stock significantly. Horse owners and breeders in the Southern and border states became the producers and salesmen of young racing prospects.

Through the transition of Thoroughbred racing from a sport that produced a small number of horses capable of running in multiple heats the same day to a more urban sport that needed a larger number of horses that could race in single dashes at much shorter distances, the Hancocks raised horses on the family farm in Virginia. They also followed the slow shift of emphasis in Thoroughbred breeding from the East Coast states to the Bluegrass region of central Kentucky. When first the prohibition of racing (through the prohibition of gambling) and then the Jersey Act wrecked the finances of the sport and breeding, the second generation found avenues to persevere in Thoroughbreds.

Through the use of stallion syndication and the overpowering strength of the American economy after World War II, the Hancocks participated in the expansion of breeding from exclusive, homebreeding operations to what have become essentially agricultural corporations that involve vast sums of money and sizable staffs of people.

As independent breeders of Thoroughbreds, as salesmen and promoters, as innovators and as conservators of racing and breeding, four generations of the Hancock family have played an interesting and vital role in the development of the Thoroughbred.

This is so because, while men of wealth and prestige have come and gone, the great breeders have lived on. Year to year and season to season, they have taken the most basic of elements, good land and good husbandry, and bred from these some of the fleetest and finest Thoroughbreds.

However, when Capt. Richard Hancock married Thomasia Harris in 1864 near the end of the conflict, their chief concern was survival, not breeding fast horses. But on Ellerslie plantation in Virginia, breeding horses came as naturally as breathing, and before long, the stock bred by Hancock was making a name for itself in racing.

Prior to the war, the premier racing in America had been heat racing, with horses trained to race against one another to win the best two of three heats at distances up to four miles. However, after 1865, dash races consisting of a single heat became the fashion, most especially in the center of industrial development, economic wealth, and racing drama: New York City.

Although increasingly rare, heat racing continued to the end of the century, but the most prestigious and valuable races were dashes. Whereas the horses sturdy enough to compete in heats at two, three, and four miles were mature animals, dash racing favored the use of younger animals. At the end of the 19th century and through the early part of the 20th century, the richest race in America was the Futurity Stakes in New York run for two-year-olds.

As racing altered to fit a different social and economic scheme, the bloodlines and physiques of the horses altered as well. Stallions and mares were imported from England to add more speed and precocity to American pedigrees, and among the best of these were the imported sires Bonnie Scotland and Leamington.

Despite Lexington's domination of American breeding from 1861 to the end of the 1870s, somewhat different bloodlines rose to prominence as the American classics were instituted in the 1870s, and the recognition of speed played a part in the rise to prominence of Ellerslie. The first nationally important sire to stand at Ellerslie was the Leamington horse Eolus, who begot the 1884 Preakness winner Knight of Ellerslie. Eolus also sired Morello, winner of the Futurity Stakes in 1892.

Those successes were important in establishing Ellerslie as a Thoroughbred nursery of national importance and in making Capt. Hancock a breeder of Thoroughbreds who earned a majority of his income from his horse sales. Even so, Ellerslie was a farm still producing a variety of crops, even if horses were its core.

Breeding farms of the late 19th and early 20th centuries were considerably different from the ones we are familiar with nowadays. Instead of standing a selection of stallions, boarding mares, and working with a variety of owners from across the nation and the world, farms of the late 19th century typically stood one or two stallions wholly owned by the farm and bred all their mares to the farm stallion. Absentee owner-breeders were rare, and the horse farmers in Virginia and Kentucky sold their entire yearling crops (or nearly all) at auctions in New York.

This process required a Thoroughbred breeder to be a man of many qualities. If a good farmer failed to market his yearlings well or build relationships with purchasers, he could go broke. Raising Thoroughbreds using home stallions was also an uncertain endeavor because a bad choice in a stallion or miscues in raising the young stock could literally bankrupt a farm in the course of a few years.

With practical considerations of this magnitude, most of the Hancocks' five sons went into more stable professions.

The Hancocks' fourth son was Arthur, however, and he became the next generation's horse breeder. Well educated, he decided against a career as an engineer and instead became his father's partner at Ellerslie.

The partnership prospered, but good and bad events lay ahead.

The most pleasant change came when the younger Hancock married Nancy Clay of Paris, Ky., in June of 1908. That was also the year that the Hart-Agnew bill effectively closed down racing in New York, the center of American racing after the War Between the States.

The result of reform legislation that swept the country – resulting in good and bad, practical and impractical changes in the laws – the Hart-Agnew bill didn't forbid racing. Instead, it outlawed bookmakers and other types of betting in New York, cutting off a primary source of revenue to the racetracks. Some other states also followed the pattern of restricting or forbidding gambling on horse races.

With the closure of racing in New York and several other states, breeding was thrown into disarray. Many horse owners and breeders panicked, dumping thousands of horses onto the market and further depressing low prices. Major breeders sent entire crops of yearlings abroad to France, England, and Argentina.

At the time, James Ben Ali Haggin was the country's largest breeder of Thoroughbreds, with nearly 500 broodmares who produced approximately 350 foals annually at Elmendorf Farm in Kentucky and Rancho del Paso in California. He was one of the leading sellers, sending shipments of breeding stock and young horses to Argentina, Germany, France, Austria, Belgium, . . . and England.

In 1908-1909, Haggin dumped more than 300 broodmares and broodmare prospects. In 1910, he sent 150 mares empty to Argentina so that they could be sold and covered back on a Southern Hemisphere schedule. Although the scale of Haggin's reduction made headlines, many other owners were just as intent on freeing themselves of horses when there was no home market for the stock.

These mass exportations led to the Jersey Act, which the English Jockey Club used to bar horses from its registry unless they traced in all lines to horses already registered in its Stud Book.

At the same time that many breeders and owners were getting out of the Thoroughbred business, the Hancocks were trying to find ways to cope with this adversity, clearly believing that better and saner days lay ahead.

While weathering the economic catastrophe caused by anti-gambling legislation in the first decade of the 20th century, Arthur Hancock leased the high-class racehorse Celt from James R. Keene. A son of Commando, Celt was born the same year as Keene's unbeaten Colin and August Belmont's high-class Fair Play, who was Colin's chief antagonist. Celt was close to them, even winning the Brooklyn Handicap from Fair Play. Upon retirement, he initially stood at Castleton in 1910, then stood at Ellerslie in 1911 and 1912 on a profit-sharing lease. Not long after the lease expired, Keene died, and Hancock was able to buy the young stallion for $25,000 from the dispersal of the Castleton Farm bloodstock in September of 1913.

Only a year before, the stallion would have sold for only a fraction of that sum if Keene had been willing to part with the horse at all. Horsemen turned out and paid good money for the Castleton Farm stock, and in part that increased optimism was caused by the fact that racing had returned to New York in the spring of 1913.

Although Celt returned to Ellerslie for the 1914 season, Arthur and Nancy Hancock had moved to Kentucky so that he could oversee the development and ensure the prosperity of land that his wife had inherited due to the premature death of her parents.

This land, lying along the Paris-Winchester Pike, the couple named Claiborne.

Capt. Hancock died in 1912, and this placed Arthur in charge of the home farm, as well as the operation in Kentucky. Celt remained at the head of the Ellerslie stud, and in search of a second to him, Hancock purchased Wrack from Lord Rosebery in England.

With the Jersey Act, many American-bred racers were only "half-bred" by the rules of the English Jockey Club. This made them essentially worthless for sale anywhere outside the U.S., and breeders with an eye to the future began to import more foreign bloodstock. Wrack was one of dozens of English-bred stallions brought over for American studs in the years following the Jersey Act.

A pretty useful stallion, Wrack sired Blazes (winner of the Harford Handicap), Careful (winner of the Laurel Handicap, Black Eyed

Susan Stakes, etc.), Flambino (Gazelle, third in Belmont Stakes, and later dam of Triple Crown winner Omaha), Fair Star (Pimlico Futurity), Petee-Wrack (Travers Stakes, Metropolitan and Suburban handicaps), and Single Foot (Brooklyn Handicap), among 31 stakes winners.

In addition to importing a steady stream of English stock, Hancock also purchased an occasional "half-bred" mare condemned by the Jersey Act. His best purchase of this sort was the Sir Martin mare Venturesome, who was carrying a foal later named Risky. As a broodmare, Risky produced Risque (Spinaway, Alabama), and Risky's best daughter at stud, Risk, produced Danger Point (Metropolitan Handicap), Sky Larking (Hopeful), Little Risk (Correction Handicap), and Beaugay (champion two-year-old filly in 1945, Arlington Lassie, Matron Stakes).

The domestic horses had also continued their successes. Celt sired Dunboyne, winner of the 1918 Futurity, as well as Celandria (Demoiselle Stakes), Coquette (Clover Stakes), Embroidery (Louisville Cup), and many other winners. Unfortunately, Celt died in 1919, at age 14.

Celt's most famous daughter is Marguerite, dam of Triple Crown winner Gallant Fox, English highweight Foxbrough (Middle Park Stakes), Fighting Fox (Wood Memorial, Massachusetts and Carter handicaps), and Petee-Wrack. Hancock bred the last-named colt, but the others were bred by William Woodward's Belair Stud and were all by a French-bred stallion named Sir Gallahad III.

Hancock's acquaintance with such elite stock was a natural development of his goals as a Thoroughbred breeder. As he was setting up Claiborne and maintaining Ellerslie, Hancock was a regular buyer of breeding stock, especially mares, at sales. One of these chance acquisitions provided an introduction to a man who was instrumental to making the Hancock breeding operations a world power.

Hancock met William Woodward after receiving a letter from the banker and owner of Belair Stud, asking to purchase a mare. Hancock had outbid Woodward's representative, and Woodward asked to purchase her. Hancock resold the mare for the purchase price and a season to Wrack, and the best bloodstock man and perhaps the most powerful investment banker in America became friends.

While the Hancock family at Ellerslie and Claiborne had become important breeders in America, producing good racing stock and prospering over the decades, Arthur Hancock had never had the financial reserves to buy some of the horses, especially the stallions, that he really wanted. But as he broadened his connections to men of great wealth who also had an interest in breeding and racing, Hancock was poised to become a Thoroughbred breeder of international importance.

Hancock knew breeding and horses and management. Woodward knew finance and international relations. Through personal associations and resulting friendships, Hancock came to know many men of wealth who wanted to race or breed good horses. Through the 1930s and 1940s, perhaps none was more enthusiastic than Woodward. Together, Hancock and Woodward formed an amazing symbiotic relationship in the production of Triple Crown winners, champions, and racers at the highest level on both sides of the Atlantic.

Together early on, they bought Jim Gaffney, from whom Claiborne bred 1923 Preakness winner Vigil. They also bought Ambassador IV. From him, Hancock bred St. James, winner of the 1923 Futurity Stakes for George Widener, and Woodward bred Priscilla Ruley, who won the Alabama Stakes at Saratoga in 1924.

However, the novelty of international racing led to Hancock and Woodward acquiring their most important sire to date. The French colt Epinard came to the U.S. and competed in three International Specials during the fall of 1924, finishing second in each but acquitting himself with distinction. Apparently, the continental champion's consistency against American competition confirmed Hancock's belief that a very fast colt who had beaten Epinard would be just his kind of stallion.

That horse was Sir Gallahad III.

**SIR GALLAHAD III**

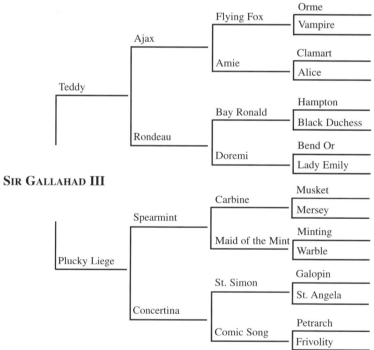

After several inquiries to owner Jefferson Davis Cohn or his agents, in the fall of 1925, the British Bloodstock Agency finally got a price on the stallion: 25,000 guineas, which was approximately $125,000 at the time. Hancock conferred with Woodward, who confirmed his interest. For an investment of this size, Hancock also brought in Marshall Field and Robert Fairbairn, making a sort of four-cornered partnership or syndicate.

After personally travelling to France and inspecting the horse at Haras de Bois Roussel, Hancock completed the deal for the young son of Teddy, and Sir Gallahad III shipped to America in December of 1925.

A roaring success from the start, Sir Gallahad III became one of the best stallions of the century. From his first crop in America came Gallant Fox, who won the Triple Crown for Woodward in 1930. And, after his retirement to stud at Claiborne, Gallant Fox sired 1935 Triple Crown winner Omaha and the 1936 Horse of the Year, Granville. Both were bred by Woodward and raced in his colors.

In addition to the stallion's ability to sire classic performers, speed was the essence that Hancock sought for in his purchase. He told Charlie Hatton in 1945 that "Sir Gallahad was the easiest of prospective sires to pick. He made the Cambridgeshire start appear a false one, and he proved quicker than Epinard."

An uncommonly potent and vigorous stallion, Sir Gallahad III sired the additional Kentucky Derby winners Hoop Jr. and Gallahadian, Preakness winner High Quest, Futurity winner Tintagel, Alabama winner Escutcheon, Travers winner Fenelon, and Vagrancy, winner of the CCA Oaks, Alabama, Beldame, and Test. Moreover, he became the leading broodmare sire in the U.S. for 12 years, as his multitude of daughters produced an army of racers and winners.

Eleven years after importing Sir Gallahad III, Hancock and a larger group of breeders purchased the 1930 English Derby winner Blenheim, already the sire of 1936 English Derby winner Mahmoud, from the Aga Khan for 45,000 pounds. William du Pont, Marion du Pont, Jock Whitney, John Hertz, and Robert Fairbairn joined Hancock as equal shareholders in the stallion, with Warren Wright taking a double share. The latter was repaid most quickly and emphatically with 1941 Triple Crown winner Whirlaway, born in Blenheim's first American crop.

As the commercial market in Thoroughbreds broadened and deepened during the middle decades of the 20th century, Hancock had proven a legendary salesman. He sold his stock on "Hancock night" at the sales, and enough of his yearlings turned out to be good racehorses to keep the demand for Claiborne stock high. The elder Hancock was leading breeder by number of races won nine times in the years beginning 1935 through 1946, and he led the nation's breeders by money won in 1935 through 1937, in 1939, and in 1943.

In all, Arthur Hancock the elder bred 138 stakes winners, including the Kentucky Derby winners Johnstown and Jet Pilot.

When World War II interrupted the transportation of Kentucky yearlings to the traditional sales at Saratoga, Hancock joined other breeders in forming the Breeders' Sales Company, which held its first auction on the grounds at Keeneland in 1943.

During that time, Hancock's son had been out of Kentucky on war duty, and when A.B. Hancock Jr. left the Air Force, he spent his energies working with both Claiborne in Kentucky and Ellerslie in Virginia.

When the Virginia property was sold in 1946, the Hancocks were now concentrating solely on Kentucky. A new tide was coming in.

Bull Hancock held a management role at Claiborne until his father fell ill in 1948, when circumstances required the son to make some decisions previously made only by his father.

Although frequently in poor health, the elder Hancock lived on until 1957, but from the late 1940s, his son Bull Hancock undertook increasingly more responsibility in managing the farm and making decisions about Claiborne. As Hugh McGuire wrote in the *Daily Racing Form* obituary for the elder Hancock, "Even though he was inactive in late years and his son, Arthur B. Hancock Jr., carried on the farm's business, the farm remained in the senior's name, as the younger Hancock said it always would, until his [father's] death."

This time of transition was one filled with difficulties, as Bull Hancock began the tasks of rejuvenating the Claiborne stallion roster and broodmare band. But the period also held great promise for the future as the years of apprenticeship under his father and the years of working around great breeding stock began to bear fruit in the selections that Hancock made to replenish Claiborne.

The story of Claiborne under Bull Hancock begins with these momentous decisions as he laid the foundations for decades of success for the farm and his family.

# CHAPTER ONE

# Foundation of the Future

*Arthur B. "Bull" Hancock was anxious. He was expecting a telegram. He had been sending and receiving them on a regular basis for months as he sought out mares and stallions, but this particular telegram would mean a lot for the future he hoped for at Claiborne Farm, the future he wanted to build with the best bloodstock he could find. But he knew it would not be a simple matter to complete this deal.*

He had heard that Nasrullah was for sale.

A foal of 1940 from the first crop by the unbeaten European racehorse Nearco, Nasrullah was the first indication of how deep and important an effect Nearco was to have on the Thoroughbred breed. A well-made but somewhat leggy colt at two, Nasrullah was the high-weighted colt on the English Free Handicap for juveniles in 1942.

In the opinion of Phil Bull, founder of the *Timeform* publishing and racing information services, Nasrullah was a man among boys. He had all the natural ability and physical components of a classic racehorse, which is what Bull thought the colt would become the next season. When returned to racing at three, Nasrullah immediately showed that he had grown into a smooth and high-quality racing animal.

Fine as he looked, Nasrullah was even more talented. He tended to toy with his opponents, not showing them much respect or consideration. This was also true, unfortunately, about his attitude to the people handling him and perhaps to racing in general.

Although Nasrullah showed his undoubted athletic ability to take the lead in both the 2,000 Guineas and the wartime Derby – both run at Newmarket – the handsome but erratic colt then declined to keep up his efforts, finishing fourth in the Guineas, third in the Derby.

After winning the Champion Stakes at Newmarket at year's end when he produced to get the lead very near the end of the race, Nasrullah was sent to stud. In the season's annual commentary published by *Timeform*, Bull's comment was, "If conformation and innate ability count for anything he may make the name for himself as a stallion which his unfortunate temperament prevented his making for himself as a racehorse."

Even Phil Bull could not have known how true that estimation would prove.

The Hancocks had kept an eye on European form and the quality of the racing and breeding stock there for nearly as long as they had bred horses. Bull Hancock liked the qualities he found in Nasrullah: the speed, the early maturity, the ability to race well in the classics, as well as the colt's exceptional family.

Bred by the Aga Khan, Nasrullah descended from the Aga Khan's landmark broodmare Mumtaz Begum in female line and in the male line from the very fast Phalaris horse Pharos through his unbeaten son Nearco, bred by Federico Tesio. Sold to Martin Benson to stand at Beech House Stud in England, Nearco was not immediately to everyone's taste as a sire.

In general, the Europeans were more impressed by Nasrullah's female family than his sire line at the time of his retirement. Worship of Nearco came only after the horse had proven beyond doubt the value of himself and his male line.

Some who bred racehorses said that Nearco was too fast and that his stock wouldn't stay. Indeed, some of them did not stay. But as Tesio, the Aga Khan, and Hancock had learned, speed kills . . . the opposition.

And those horses who have plenty of natural speed and the ability to go middle distances are much above average as breeding prospects.

Perhaps part of breeders' concerns about Nasrullah as a breeding prospect also came from his illustrious female family. He was out of the

Blenheim mare Mumtaz Begum, who was a daughter of the famous Mumtaz Mahal. The Flying Filly herself was a tremendous physical specimen, and she reproduced the qualities of her physique on the racetrack.

The gray sold for 9,100 guineas at the Doncaster yearling sales in 1922, when George Lambton made the first exceptional purchases that laid the foundation of the Aga Khan's breeding and racing empire. Mumtaz Mahal won seven of her 10 starts, was the highweight juvenile of 1923 over colts, and her family bred on to produce outstanding racehorses, exceptional broodmares, and sires of international importance for decades.

Among the leading stallions descending from her are Nasrullah, Mahmoud, and Royal Charger.

Nasrullah was out of Mumtaz Mahal's daughter Mumtaz Begum, by the Epsom Derby winner Blenheim. A horse of great quality and natural energy, Blenheim was a very important sire in Europe, siring Epsom Derby winner Mahmoud, among others, and then a syndicate put together by the elder A.B. Hancock purchased the stallion to stand at Claiborne.

From his first Kentucky crop, Blenheim sired Triple Crown winner Whirlaway for the Calumet Farm of Warren Wright, who had taken two of the eight shares in the stallion. Calumet reaped most of the immediate rewards from the importation of Blenheim, also breeding and racing the Kentucky Oaks winner Nellie L. and champion handicap mare Mar-Kell. Calumet also bred two champions (Coaltown and Wistful) and two Kentucky Derby winners (Ponder and Hill Gail) from the daughters of Blenheim.

Blenheim was the leading sire in the U.S. in 1941, when Whirlaway won the Triple Crown, and the chestnut colt quickly replaced Seabiscuit as America's leading money winner. In all, Blenheim sired 61 stakes winners from 536 foals in the U.S. and Europe and made a lasting contribution of quality to the breed.

Among Blenheim's many successful racers was Jet Pilot, winner of the 1947 Kentucky Derby. The chestnut colt was bred by A.B. Hancock Sr. in partnership with Mrs. R.A. Van Clief.

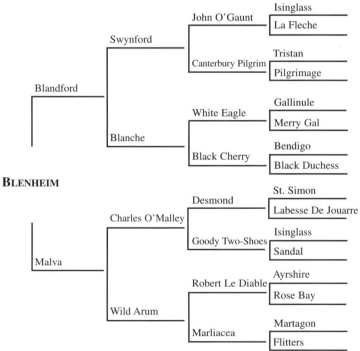

**BLENHEIM**

- Blandford
  - Swynford
    - John O'Gaunt
      - Isinglass
      - La Fleche
    - Canterbury Pilgrim
      - Tristan
      - Pilgrimage
  - Blanche
    - White Eagle
      - Gallinule
      - Merry Gal
    - Black Cherry
      - Bendigo
      - Black Duchess
- Malva
  - Charles O'Malley
    - Desmond
      - St. Simon
      - Labesse De Jouarre
    - Goody Two-Shoes
      - Isinglass
      - Sandal
  - Wild Arum
    - Robert Le Diable
      - Ayrshire
      - Rose Bay
    - Marliacea
      - Martagon
      - Flitters

By the time that Bull Hancock was working to buy Blenheim's grandson Nasrullah, the stallion had been at Claiborne more than a dozen years. The depth of family and the Claiborne connections would certainly have kept Bull Hancock's interest high in Nasrullah. After the end of Nasrullah's racing career, Hancock tried to buy him but could not get it done until 1950. By then, Nasrullah had become a proven sire in Europe, as well as in America, where his Irish-bred son Noor had raced with such distinction that he even defeated Citation (then a five-year-old).

## Nasrullah's Arrival

Getting a new stallion is like Christmas to horse breeders, but getting a grand animal like Nasrullah was Christmas times ten. The stallion that Joe Estes characterized as having a "diamond-studded pedigree and the disposition of a paranoid mule" had the racing ability to match his pedigree, and he had already shown he was a significant stallion. All that Hancock had to do was get him to the farm.

The actual purchase proved more intricate than Hancock, perhaps, had bargained on. Arthur Hancock III recalled that "there was a hiccup in the deal to purchase Nasrullah."

Fortunately, his father was able to call on the right sort of man to relieve the problem. "My mother's father was an attorney in Nashville," Arthur Hancock said, "and I know they went to New York together" to work out the details of the purchase.

The sticking point probably arose because Nasrullah was gaining greater successes almost daily between the time the original agreement had been made in December 1949 and the time it was consummated in New York. Whether it was a question of pressure from breeders at home in Europe or some degree of seller's remorse, Joseph McGrath, who owned Nasrullah at the time, was having trouble concluding the transaction.

Hancock said, "They had a deal done, and then Mr. McGrath was not gonna go through with it. And Seth Walker, who was my grandfather, told him, 'I've got several Irishmen in my country, and in Tennessee, an Irishman always keeps his word. We've done this deal. Are you telling us now that you're going to renege on your word?' And that got it done.

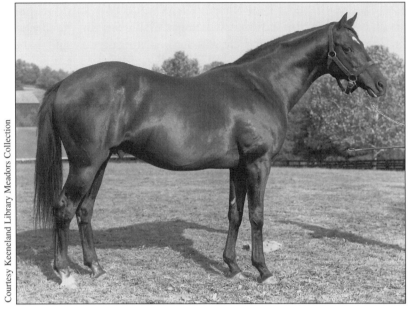

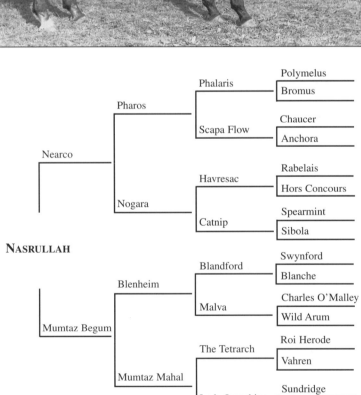

**NASRULLAH**

Nearco
  Pharos
    Phalaris
      Polymelus
      Bromus
    Scapa Flow
      Chaucer
      Anchora
  Nogara
    Havresac
      Rabelais
      Hors Concours
    Catnip
      Spearmint
      Sibola

Mumtaz Begum
  Blenheim
    Blandford
      Swynford
      Blanche
    Malva
      Charles O'Malley
      Wild Arum
  Mumtaz Mahal
    The Tetrarch
      Roi Herode
      Vahren
    Lady Josephine
      Sundridge
      Americus Girl

It shook him so much that they got the deal done, and they brought him over here."

The principal reasons that Hancock wanted Nasrullah were obvious: "Daddy wanted him because he was an outcross and looked like he was getting runners," Arthur Hancock said. "And there was nothing really from the Nearco line over here at the time. I think there was one horse, but he wanted that line, too. I think Daddy met Nasrullah in New York and came in on the train with him. I remember Daddy gettin' off the train. He had his overalls on."

Nasrullah arrived at Claiborne in early July 1950 after a 14-day journey from Ireland by ship and then by train from New York. Arthur Hancock, even as a boy, sensed the significance of the horse's arrival.

"I remember Nasrullah coming in down there" at the train station in Paris, Ky., which is about a mile from the Claiborne Farm entrance. "My mother's got films of him arriving on the train. I remember Princequillo coming in, Double Jay." Their arrivals were all the more important because they were the turning of the tide in the fortunes of Claiborne Farm "because my grandfather had had the strokes," which kept him from managing the farm as he had in years past, and "Daddy had to build it up again," Arthur said.

So even from the point of view of a young boy, the arrival of the hottest young stallion in the world was major news. It was also a turn of events that would mean so much to the future of Claiborne Farm.

In addition to ratcheting up the caliber of stallions at the farm, the Hancocks had made the decision to concentrate solely on Claiborne and had sold the property in Virginia called Ellerslie. This decision had been a long time coming, but history and family ties kept the land in their hands long past the time when it would have been convenient to sell it off.

In a 1939 census of the Hancock holdings of land and bloodstock prior to the Second World War, Claiborne was at 2,100 acres, with 13 stallions. Hancock Sr. owned 75 broodmares and had 120 mares as boarders in Kentucky. In contrast, at Ellerslie, there were only three stallions, with 26 mares owned by Hancock and 18 boarders.

The balance of power between the Kentucky and Virginia operations had irrevocably shifted in favor of Claiborne. Yet the eldest Arthur Hancock, seemingly for reasons of sentiment and historical ties, had held onto the family's original land and seat of success.

Even though he had retained Ellerslie over the decades, the difficulties of managing both it and Claiborne had taxed the elder Hancock. Although Bull Hancock was able to shoulder some of the responsibility of management, his father was accustomed to making all the decisions on the farms, and the elder Hancock did not have the reputation as the easiest man to work for. But circumstances beyond the control of either powerful and determined man were going to take a large part in resolving the problems of distant farms and intense personalities.

Beginning in the early 1940s, the demands of World War II called Bull Hancock away from his destination at Claiborne Farm. When the war was over, it was an event that created strong memories, as even a very young Arthur Hancock III recalled his father's return.

"I was born in '43," he said, "and I can remember him coming back from the war in uniform." That happy homecoming was none too soon for the needs of Claiborne and Ellerslie. Both were under the supervision of the elder Hancock, but time and health troubles were keeping him from managing with the energy of his youth and middle age.

Furthermore, the war effort had taken enormous amounts of cash and supplies, as well as most of the American labor supply, and farms were hit even harder than other businesses. "I can remember coming back from Nashville" [where young Arthur and his mother Waddell had stayed with her family], Arthur Hancock III recalled, "and the grass in front of Claiborne House was really tall."

With the combination of labor shortages and encroaching age, some things did not receive the sort of attention during the war years and immediately thereafter that they would have in decades past. Tires, gasoline, and other war-related items were rationed to the general public. Prices declined for yearlings, stallion fees had to be reduced in accord, fewer yearlings were bred and sold, and income to the breeding farms was lower. But changes in response to these problems and other concerns came slowly in the Hancock dominions, partly because the family's patriarch was accustomed to ruling his domain, not being ruled by circumstance.

Arthur Hancock had been solely on his own in business since his father's death in 1912, had restored Ellerslie to the height of its reputation with the acquisition of Celt, had built Claiborne entirely on his own initiative and insight into the most important breeding operation in the country, and had little regard for the inclinations of others. He was used to doing it his way.

Age and infirmity, however, have no respect for individuals or accomplishments. The elder Hancock's first stroke came in 1948. He died in 1957, and his health had been poor to bad all the years in between.

Courtesy Keeneland Library Meadors Collection

Arthur "Bull" Hancock, Jr. and his father confer at Claiborne

After the first blow to his father's health, Bull Hancock became much more involved in managing Claiborne. Ellerslie had been sold a couple of years earlier, and that decision provided a decrease of management worries and also a good infusion of cash into Claiborne.

This financial boost had to have helped as Bull Hancock began the task of rebuilding the broodmare band and stallion corps. To do this, Hancock had to be ruthless about culling.

Arthur Hancock said, "I can recall from what my daddy told me that as my grandfather got older, he let the broodmare band go down. He didn't buy more really good mares. The stallions had pretty well fallen off."

By 1950, Blenheim was 23, and Sir Gallahad III had died the year before. So the farm's lineup of stallions was needing some premium replacements, as well as fresh blood in the broodmare band.

"I remember Daddy telling me that he came back from the army and went through the broodmares in all the barns at Claiborne," Arthur Hancock said. "He walked through there and looked at 'em all. One story he told . . . they had a mare named Black Rage there, and she was a real bad mare, would get you. He went in the stall with her and petted her and looked at her foal. And the next morning, he said to Harris Robertson, who was the manager then, 'I went through and looked at all the mares yesterday. Saw 'em all.'

"Harris said, 'You didn't go in the stall with Black Rage, did you?'

"He said, 'Yep. She was fine.'

"Harris said, 'She's a killer. She's really bad.'

"So Daddy said, 'Well, I'll show you.'

"So they drove back to the barn, and he went to go in the stall with her, and she just came at him with her teeth bared, whirled around and kicked. He always figured she knew by that time he was cautious of her, afraid of her. Or maybe it was because Harris was with him. Horses are funny. They don't like certain people."

Black Rage (1938, Neddie - Sunayr by *Sun Briar) was sent off the farm in 1948. By 1950, Hancock had culled more than two dozen of the Claiborne broodmares and was working to acquire better replacement stock.

# Change for the Better

When assuming the greater duties of running Claiborne, Bull Hancock confided some of his thoughts to *Daily Racing Form's* bloodstock columnist Charlie Hatton, with Hancock noting that he was "unhappy with certain aspects of the farm's aims and most of its mares."

Hatton quoted Hancock saying that "we haven't replaced any stock in 12 years. We have about 75 mares, and I don't like any of them except two. I would like to upgrade the mares and instead of breeding for speed and precocity, try to produce potential classic horses like Gallant Fox."

Due to factors beyond the control of A.B. Hancock, Sr., Claiborne had become stagnant in that period, although it was a time of great change in racing. After the Depression of the 1930s, however, even the privation of the war years wasn't terrible, and some things had changed for the better. Purses had more than doubled from 1939 to the early 1950s, while the foal crop had risen only 50 percent.

That change in the ratio of earnings to runners was immensely important, and Bull Hancock wanted to take advantage of that opportunity, as well as benefit from the improvements he was making in the breeding stock at Claiborne. Writing in 1953, Charlie Hatton noted in *Daily Racing Form* that in the "last few years, nearly a 100 percent turnover of Claiborne mares has taken place. They have been replaced by new mares from the Claiborne 'filly' racing stable, and by purchases here and abroad." The average age of the new mares at Claiborne was nine, and the majority of the new mares' first foals arrived in the 1952 foal crop.

The mares and foals of the 1952 crop were a watershed in many regards. For one thing, these young horses included the first foals by Nasrullah since his importation to Claiborne, as well as the first foals from many of Hancock's new replacement mares.

Among the mares to produce their first foals for Claiborne in 1952 were Bourtai, Rough Shod, and Knight's Daughter. Only three of many good mares that Claiborne acquired in the early 1950s, these three were ancestors of many of the most exciting racehorses that the farm bred over the next couple of decades.

Bourtai, for instance, was part of a private purchase that Hancock engineered in 1951. He purchased all nine of Sylvester Labrot's broodmares boarded at Claiborne, including Bourtai. There was a lot of Claiborne history with this mare, since Labrot had purchased her as a yearling at the Keeneland sales for $5,500 from Claiborne client Marshall Field. Furthermore, Bourtai was in foal to Nasrullah at the time of sale, carrying a filly later named Delta.

A stakes winner from the first American crop by Nasrullah, Delta won the Arlington Lassie and was second in the Arlington Futurity. She won more stakes at four, then developed into an exceptional producer for Claiborne Farm. Delta became a landmark producer for Claiborne, and not for another breeder's operation, because, in a dramatic development in 1953, Hancock decided not to auction Claiborne's yearling crop. He told Charlie Hatton that "it was virtually impossible to race part of our yearlings and have buyers' acceptance for the remainder sold at auction."

As a result, Hancock sold a portion of the most marketable yearlings privately and retained the rest for racing. At least 20 yearlings of the 1953 crop sold privately, including four Nasrullahs, three Princequillos, two Blenheims, and one by Count Fleet. A half-dozen of the yearlings went to Christopher Chenery, with others sold to Howell Jackson, Melville Church, Lord Astor, and Gordon Guiberson.

Among the ones sold was the Nasrullah colt Blue Ruler, a highly regarded stakes winner at two whose victories included the Del Mar Futurity, and Blue Ruler was one of the yearlings sold to Guiberson. He later resold them to Murcain Stable, owned by Mrs. Clint Murchison and Mrs. Wofford Cain, and for them, Blue Ruler won four of his seven starts as a juvenile.

Among the ones Hancock kept, the best race filly was Delta, a stakes winner whose victories included the Arlington Lassie, and after her retirement to stud, she became an important broodmare. From 10 foals, Delta produced five stakes winners and another stakes-placed filly. The best of them was the Herbager colt Dike, who came closer to giving Bull Hancock his career goal of a victory in the Kentucky Derby than any other horse.

Delta

Choosing to keep a significant portion of his young stock and race them was a remarkable move, both in its timing and in the effect it produced in making Claiborne one of the country's most important owners, as well as an important breeder.

But for an operation that was not based on great wealth created in another sphere, such as banking, oil, or industry, becoming an owner-breeder on a national scale was a tremendous risk. The 1953 yearling crop was only the second Hancock-bred crop of yearlings since 1886 that had not been sold at public auction, and the only previous exception had been when the entire crop of yearlings, all by Celt, had been sold privately to A.H. Waterman.

Part of the reason for the change, Hancock explained, was that "we want to race a few horses, but not all the horses that we raise. Therefore, we have sold a few yearlings privately." By selling a number of yearlings privately, Hancock was able to show interested buyers that the ones available were not culls and was better able to dictate into whose hands the young horses went. And the decision also left Claiborne able to retain racing stock to pursue larger goals in the sport.

Also part of the rationale for the change was the growth of purses and the earnings that horses could accumulate. Combined, these factors encouraged Hancock to take the plunge into a large racing stable.

Hatton wrote "the 1953 yearling crop was to have been the full unveiling of the intensive rebuilding program that has been undertaken at Claiborne." In addition to younger and better broodmares, the farm now stood Nasrullah, whose fame in the U.S. and success abroad had only increased during the time from his importation to Claiborne and his first yearlings' appearance on the sales scene.

The top juvenile of his year and third in the Derby, Nasrullah was an outstanding racehorse with a questionable temperament. Although Nasrullah was well-known for antics before the start of some of his races, the horse raced well enough, and Phil Bull noted that Nasrullah was reliable and game, but only until he took the lead. Then, apparently, he thought his job was done.

While he had put up some first-class performances on the race-track, not everyone was enthralled with Nasrullah as a stallion. But when his runners began to show their ability, no careful reader of form could doubt that this was a stallion of considerable worth.

Bob Courtney, owner of Crestfield Farm in Lexington, Ky., recalled that the importation of Nasrullah was a momentous occasion among local breeders. He said, "When Nasrullah first was imported, the talk on the street was focused on wondering why the English would let the horse go, but once he got started on the racetrack, he set the world afire. On the farm, Nasrullah was surely a handful to work with. He'd get up on his hindlegs and take out lightbulbs or anything else, but man, he was some kind of sire."

The year before Bull Hancock purchased Nasrullah, the stallion's daughter Musidora had won the 1,000 Guineas and Oaks in England. His son Noor had raced into third place in the 1948 Derby at Epsom, and after his importation to race in the U.S. for Charles Howard (the owner of Seabiscuit), Noor won the Santa Anita Handicap in early 1950, which significantly increased breeders' interest in the new stallion destined for Kentucky. After Hancock had imported the stallion to Claiborne in mid-1950, Nasrullah became utterly golden.

Noor won the Hollywood Gold Cup in the summer of 1950. Belle of All showed herself to be the best English juvenile filly with a victory in the Cheveley Park Stakes. The following year, 1951, Belle of All won the 1,000 Guineas. So Nasrullah had his second classic-winning filly while standing his first season in the States. In 1952, Nasrullah's son Nearula was the highweighted juvenile colt, and he carried on that form to his three-year-old season and a victory in the 2,000 Guineas at Newmarket in 1953. In addition to all these classic racers, Nasrullah had sired several other good stakes winners, including the high-class sprinter Grey Sovereign, who became a very good sire in Europe, as well.

But on the European stage, Nasrullah saved his best for last.

In his last crop sired in Ireland, Nasrullah got Never Say Die from the War Admiral mare Singing Grass. Robert Sterling Clark brought Singing Grass from Ireland to the States while carrying Never Say Die. The horse was thus an American-bred who returned to England for his great successes.

Racing for Clark, the handsome chestnut colt won the 1954 Derby and St. Leger, proving beyond any doubt that Nasrullah could sire a colt with the stamina for classic success. In England's longest classic, the St. Leger at Doncaster, Never Say Die dominated the field, winning off by a dozen lengths.

The continuing success of Nasrullah's stock at all distances, but more especially the mounting prestige of their accomplishments, combined to make the young son of Nearco the most sought-after stallion in America through the rest of the 1950s.

The year of Never Say Die's Derby victory, 1954, a yearling from Nasrullah's second American crop sold for a record yearling sale price of $80,000, and in each of the next two years, a colt by Nasrullah sold at public auction for the same sum.

By choosing to leave the auction market with the Claiborne stock and to sell some and race others, Hancock missed out on the potential auction returns from Claiborne homebred yearlings. But he was able to keep many of the good horses Claiborne bred and then return them to the farm as building blocks for the next generation.

The 1953 crop of yearlings that included the first American foals by Nasrullah began to race in 1954. As soon as they raced, they started winning left and right. The best colt that Claiborne bred in Nasrullah's first crop was Blue Ruler, which the farm had sold. The best filly was Delta, and she was ranked one pound below champion High Voltage on the Experimental Free Handicap for two-year-olds in 1954. High Voltage was by Claiborne stallion Ambiorix and was bred and raced by the Wheatley Stable of Mrs. Gladys Mills Phipps, the mother of Ogden Phipps.

Other stakes winners from Nasrullah's first U.S. crop included Flying Fury (Champagne at two, Derby Trial at three), Lea Lane (Durazna Stakes at two, 2nd in the Kentucky Oaks at three), and Nashua.

Among the 1952 foal crop, the best of the Nasrullahs and the best of the two-year-olds was the big bay colt from Belair Stud named Nashua. He was bred by William Woodward Sr., who died when the colt was a yearling. Otherwise, Nashua would have been sent to race in England, where he might have followed in the footsteps of Never Say Die at Epsom or Doncaster and might even have proven a more than worthy opponent to the great Ribot, at least under certain conditions.

Hancock's decision to sell part of Claiborne's 1953 yearlings privately and retain the rest for racing began to look inspired. The 1953 Claiborne crop of yearlings included stock from the second crops of Ambiorix and Double Jay, as well as young prospects by Princequillo, Blenheim, and a handful of well-forgotten sires.

The first crop of yearlings that Hancock bred and kept also included the good fillies Delta and Courtesy. Both became bedrock broodmares for Claiborne's expansion as a national force in racing.

# A Band of Broodmares

Among the yearlings that Claiborne retained, the second crop had the champion filly Doubledogdare, by Double Jay, and the third crop had champions Round Table and Bayou.

Of these, the horse with the greatest long-term influence on Claiborne was, without a doubt, Round Table. A dark bay son of

Princequillo and the best colt that Claiborne had bred by that stallion, Round Table was the farm's chief hope for a victory in the Kentucky Derby in 1957.

Campaigned by Claiborne at two under Bull Hancock's home-bred plan, Round Table won the Breeders' Futurity at Keeneland at the end of his juvenile season. A neatly made and handy type of racer, Round Table had shown enough speed to be a challenger with two-year-olds, as well as the finishing power to carry him a distance of ground.

As an indication of Round Table's versatility and of how the American racing program has changed in the past 50 years, the horse started 10 times as a two-year-old, winning five of them. His first race was a three-furlong sprint at Hialeah near the end of February. He won his maiden and then the four-furlong Lafayette Stakes at Keeneland in April and raced well through the year to October, when he won the Breeders' Futurity at Keeneland over the Beard Course of seven furlongs 184 feet.

Despite Hancock's desire to win the Derby, he was a very practical horseman. And in February of 1957, Hancock sold the colt to Travis Kerr for a price reported as $175,000.

That season, Round Table won 15 of his 22 starts but was third in his primary objective, the Kentucky Derby. Despite an outstanding campaign at three, Round Table was one of an amazing crop of three-year-olds in 1957 that included Bold Ruler, Gallant Man, Iron Liege, and Gen. Duke. With the level of competition this group generated, Round Table's third-place finish in the Trenton Handicap late in 1957 behind both Bold Ruler and Gallant Man secured the three-year-old championship and Horse of the Year for the son of Nasrullah, Bold Ruler, who also was bred and raised at Claiborne.

Both colts raced on at four, with Bold Ruler retiring in August. Round Table raced through both 1958 and 1959, completing his four-year-old season with 14 victories from 20 starts, becoming the third horse to win more than $1 million, earning Horse of the Year in 1958, eventually passing Nashua as the world's leading money winner, and retiring to stud sound.

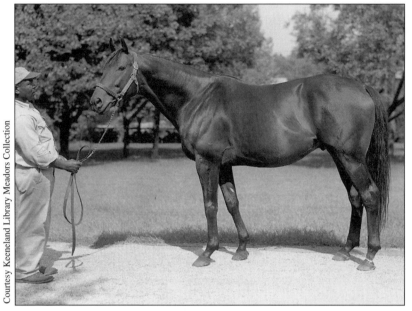

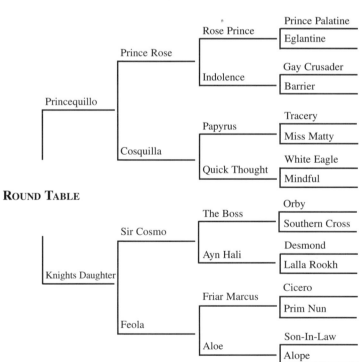

**ROUND TABLE**

Princequillo
- Prince Rose
  - Rose Prince
    - Prince Palatine
    - Eglantine
  - Indolence
    - Gay Crusader
    - Barrier
- Cosquilla
  - Papyrus
    - Tracery
    - Miss Matty
  - Quick Thought
    - White Eagle
    - Mindful

Knights Daughter
- Sir Cosmo
  - The Boss
    - Orby
    - Southern Cross
  - Ayn Hali
    - Desmond
    - Lalla Rookh
- Feola
  - Friar Marcus
    - Cicero
    - Prim Nun
  - Aloe
    - Son-In-Law
    - Alope

Although Hancock had sold Round Table near the beginning of his second season of racing, the breeder had retained a 20 percent interest in the horse as a stallion, and the son of Princequillo retired to his birthplace, where he, too, became a leading sire and broodmare sire.

With many other horses, but especially with Round Table, the result of Hancock's practice of keeping homebreds and racing them meant that Claiborne was making its own stallions, was retaining stallion prospects to retire to the farm, and was enriching its broodmare band with tremendous prospects.

And Round Table's existence was due to the band of young mares that Hancock had secured earlier in the decade. He purchased the Sir Cosmo mare Knight's Daughter in foal to Watling Street, and she produced her first American foal in 1952 at Claiborne. The Watling Street was a filly later named Yarmouth, and Hancock sold her privately in 1953. For Meadow Stable, she founded a good-quality family through her only foal, stakes winner Salt Lake, later dam of the good producer Orissa.

Knight's Daughter produced only two more foals for Claiborne, but both were major stakes winners. They were Round Table and his full sister Monarchy. Winner of the Arlington Lassie at two, Monarchy was a bit leggier and lighter than her brother, and she became a useful producer at Claiborne, with stakes winners Titled and Fabled Monarch, and stakes-placed Blade, among her produce.

In addition to Knight's Daughter, Hancock also purchased the broodmare Highway Code from Lord Astor and helped arrange the purchase of Rough Shod at Newmarket for Claiborne client Thomas Girdler.

Highway Code was no young thing when Hancock bought and imported her in 1950. A foal of 1939, Highway Code was by Hyperion out of the outstanding mare Book Law, winner of the 1927 St. Leger and descended from one of the best families in the Astor stud. Highway Code was part of Nasrullah's first book and rewarded Claiborne with a filly named Courtesy in 1952. Stakes-placed at two and three, Courtesy became a really good producer for Claiborne, and three generations later, her great-grandson Swale became the farm's first Kentucky Derby winner in 1984.

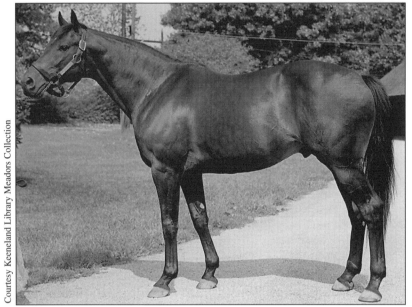

**AMBIORIX**

| | | | Chouberski |
|---|---|---|---|
| | | Bruleur | |
| | Ksar | | Basse Terre |
| | | | Omnium |
| | | Kizil Kourgan | |
| Tourbillon | | | Kasbah |
| | | | Rabelais |
| | | Durbar | |
| | Durban | | Armenia |
| | | | Irish Lad |
| | | Banshee | |
| | | | Frizette |
| | | | Polymelus |
| | | Phalaris | |
| | Pharos | | Bromus |
| | | | Chaucer |
| | | Scapa Flow | |
| Lavendula | | | Anchora |
| | | | John O'Gaunt |
| | | Swynford | |
| | Sweet Lavender | | Canterbury Pilgrim |
| | | | Marco |
| | | Marchetta | |
| | | | Hettie Sorrel |

A considerable amount of the glory that Claiborne enjoyed as an owner and breeder in the time before Swale was related to the family descending from Rough Shod. A good-sized and rather rugged mare, Rough Shod produced her first foal for Girdler at Claiborne in 1952, and it was the stakes winner Gambetta, by My Babu.

Prior to Claiborne's acquisition of Rough Shod and her stakes-winning daughter in 1961, Gambetta had already become the dam of a stakes winner and three stakes-placed horses, and she saved the best of them all for Hancock and Perry in her champion daughter Gamely.

Rough Shod, although mated to Nasrullah only once, produced all the very best offspring by his son Nantallah. This blazing brood of immensely talented racers included Ridan, winner of the 1962 Florida Derby, champion Moccasin, John B. Campbell Handicap winner Lt. Stevens, and stakes-placed Thong, who ran second in the Alcibiades.

That one mare and stallion produced so many high-class off-spring is exceptional, but that Moccasin produced European champion Apalachee (by Round Table) and six other stakes winners was extraordinary. Thong did even better. Her best racers were Grade 1 winner King Pellinore (by Round Table) and highweighted European sprinter Thatch (by Forli). Her best producing daughter was Special, dam of the internationally-renowned sire Nureyev and the high-class mares Number and Bound. Special's daughter Fairy Bridge, in turn, produced the greatest European sire of the late 20th century and early 21st century, Sadler's Wells, and his full brother Fairy King.

In addition to purchasing broodmares of lasting significance to Claiborne and the breed, Hancock also continued to add stallions to the farm. Among the European champions Hancock acquired to stand at Claiborne were Ambiorix and Tulyar. Bred in France by Marcel Boussac, Ambiorix was a very fast French racer who was the top juvenile colt in France in 1948. The next year, Ambiorix won the Prix Greffulhe and Prix Lupin and was second in the Prix du Jockey Club.

Hancock acquired Ambiorix in September 1949 and was quoted in *The Blood-Horse* saying that "I tried to buy My Babu, but they wanted too much money for him. Ambiorix was a three-parts brother to him, and a champion at two in France, so I got him for $250,000 and syndicated him pretty quick" (stallion's obituary, March 24, 1975).

There were five original syndicate members in the horse: Harry Guggenheim, the Phipps family, William Woodward Sr., Mrs. John Hertz, and Arthur Hancock Sr. The last truly important stallion from the Herod male line, Ambiorix sired champion High Voltage for Wheatley Stable in his second crop. She was his best racer, but Ambiorix continued to produce plenty of good-class stock and led the general sire list in 1960.

The daughters of Ambiorix became good producers also, and High Voltage is the dam of the top sprinter Impressive (by Court Martial) and stakes winners Great Power and Bold Commander (both by Bold Ruler), who won the Chesapeake Stakes at three. As a stallion, Bold Commander became the first son of Bold Ruler to sire a classic winner when his son Dust Commander won the 1970 Kentucky Derby. High Voltage's stakes-placed daughter Irradiate is the dam of Majestic Light, a high-class racehorse and successful sire who stood his entire career at Claiborne.

In 1955, Hancock put together a syndicate to purchase European champion Tulyar from the Irish National Stud. The National Stud had purchased Tulyar two years earlier for about $700,000 from the Aga Khan, and at the time, it was reported that an American syndicate had offered $1 million for the horse at the same time.

Unbeaten in seven starts at three, Tulyar won the Epsom Derby and set a record for a single season's earnings in England. The price that the American syndicate paid the National Stud for Tulyar was pretty stiff at 240,000 pounds (approximately $672,000 at the time), and even so, it caused a great uproar in the Irish government, since the National Stud is state-owned, and was debated in the Dáil Eireann (one of the Houses of the Irish Parliament).

As with the purchase of Nasrullah, Tulyar was sold in the fall and was not transferred to the States until the middle of the following year so the horse could fulfill the breeding contracts for him in the spring of 1956. Tulyar arrived at Claiborne in July of 1956 after an overnight airline flight from Ireland. The stallion had a short stop in New York to clear customs, then was flown on to Lexington.

Tulyar showed great character as a racehorse and continued to demonstrate personality at stud. His Irish groom Matthew Lynch noted that when Tulyar was younger "we used to feed him two quarts of Guinness stout with his mash, and he thrived on it." A level-headed disposition and his natural character made Tulyar a popular horse. Yet before Tulyar even covered a mare in America, he nearly died.

Set to begin covering in early 1957, Tulyar was removed from service due to an attack of colitis and an infection. In a story dated March 22 in *Daily Racing Form*, Bull Hancock said, "He is back on his feed. In fact, he is eating more than any other horse on the farm. He also has regained his zest, and if improvement continues at this rate, we hope to return him to his breeding schedule."

Yet the horse did not maintain the progress expected of him, and six weeks later, Tulyar was still a sick horse. His condition fluctuated from middling to poor, and the nature of his ailment baffled Hancock and the farm veterinarians.

Experts from across the country and the world consulted on the horse's condition, and Col. Floyd Sager, resident vet at Claiborne, noted that other veterinarians had concurred with the original diagnosis of colitis, and he told *Daily Racing Form* in April that "Tulyar is in his paddock and has eaten all the grain he was given." Even though this seemed positive, Sager said that the stallion's "legs are stiff and sore."

The toxic effects of the colon problems caused the horse to lose hair, as well as condition, and he looked to be in bad straits a few times. In late April of 1957, Tulyar had suffered intestinal cramps and swelling to such a degree that Hancock "didn't think he would live a week."

Tulyar showed a great will to live, springing back time after time from these problems, and in November of that year, Hancock told the *Racing Form* that he was hopeful the stallion could return to service the following year. He said, "Tulyar is still convalescing but is doing as well as we can expect, and I anticipate that he will serve 20 or 25 mares. He is within 30 pounds of his normal weight, and his coat and general appearance are very good."

**TULYAR**

| | | | Prince Chimay |
|---|---|---|---|
| | | Vatout | Vashti |
| | Bois Roussel | | Spearmint |
| | | Plucky Liege | Concertina |
| Tehran | | | Gainsborough |
| | | Solario | Sun Worship |
| | Stafaralla | | Phalaris |
| | | Mirawala | Miranda |
| | | | Phalaris |
| | | Pharos | Scapa Flow |
| | Nearco | | Havresac |
| | | Nogara | Catnip |
| Neocracy | | | Swynford |
| | | Blandford | Blanche |
| | Harina | | Farasi |
| | | Athasi | Athgreany |

The constant care and attention of the staff at Claiborne and the horse's natural constitution pulled him through the strange malady. By spring of the following year, just as Hancock had judged, Tulyar was covering mares, with 30 booked to him.

Although a tremendous racehorse himself, Tulyar was more of a hard-core European middle-distance horse than Hancock usually was inclined to purchase. His conformation, noteworthy for quality and size more than muscle power, was very well suited to European racing. From his Irish-sired crops, Tulyar got the Irish 1,000 Guineas winner Florintina and the highweighted French two-year-old filly Ginetta.

Although Tulyar did not achieve the level of success as a stallion in America that Hancock and others hoped he would, Tulyar sired 29 stakes winners in all for a highly respectable 10 percent stakes winners from foals.

The best of his American foals was champion Castle Forbes. Once again a Claiborne stallion produced his best racer for the Phipps family, and Castle Forbes was bred and raced for Wheatley Stable. Castle Forbes won the Gardenia and Sorority at two, then the Acorn at three, when she also ran second in the Coaching Club American Oaks and third in the Alabama and Beldame.

Castle Forbes produced only four foals, but three of them were high-class racers. All were by Bold Ruler. Irish Castle won the Hopeful at two, then sired Kentucky Derby and Belmont winner Bold Forbes. Alpine Lass won the Matron at two.

Another of Tulyar's stakes winners from his early crops at Claiborne was the late-maturing Margarethen, who won the Beverly Handicap at four and five, then retired to stud and produced the international champion Trillion and other good horses.

Another late-maturing daughter was Hinterland, who did not win a stakes until she was five. In all, however, she raced 78 times and went on to become a rock-solid producer. Her best offspring include Heartlight, a graded stakes winner at two going a distance on turf, and Feel the Beat, a tremendous sprinting filly who won 14 races and $640,973 in the late 1980s and early 1990s.

When Tulyar was put down in 1972 at age 23, one of his older stakes-winning daughters, Tularia, was in foal for the first time to a fast son of Bold Ruler named What a Pleasure. Their offspring was a very handsome bay colt later named Honest Pleasure. He became the champion juvenile colt of 1975 and started as an odds-on favorite for the Kentucky Derby the next year. Honest Pleasure finished second to Irish Castle's son Bold Forbes under a perfectly judged front-running ride from Angel Cordero.

The quality of Tulyar's overall record was considerably slanted in favor of his fillies, and his daughters have continued to make an impact on the breed.

Both Ambiorix and Tulyar were strongly European in type and pedigree. Hancock was clearly trying to stretch out some of the American lines to go longer distances, to win those classic races he so dearly loved.

In 1957, Hancock had a colt on his hands that gave him hope for the Derby the next year. A son of Nasrullah out of another mare Hancock had added to the Claiborne broodmare band, Nadir was a late-maturing juvenile who won the Garden State Stakes in the style of a colt who should be notably better at three.

In the Nov. 2 issue of *The Blood-Horse*, Hancock said "I would like to win a Kentucky Derby, and this might be the one to do it. He's green and he's big. He needs time, and that's why we're passing up the Pimlico Futurity."

Hancock came to own this big, green colt because he went to a lot of hard work to buy his dam, Gallita, a full sister to champion Gallorette. Both were bred by W. L. Brann and were sired by his imported Swynford stallion Challenger II from the Sir Gallahad III mare Gallette.

But whereas Gallorette was a great racemare, one of the best mares of the 20th century who had won 21 races, her full sister was only a winner of two races from 11 starts.

Hancock wanted her because she was a full sister to Gallorette and because "Ed Christmas told me she could do anything Gallorette could do, and besides that she was a grand-looking mare."

Hancock had, in 1953, tried to buy Gallita from Brann's widow but was told the eight-year-old mare was not for sale. After a bit of negotiating, Hancock wound up buying all of Brann's mares, then reselling all of them, except for Gallita.

The first of four Nasrullah foals that the mare produced for Claiborne was Nadir.

His only stakes victory at two was in the richest race of the year, the Garden State Stakes, but he did not immediately fulfill the hopes Hancock had for him at three. He didn't come to his form until midsummer with a victory in the American Derby, and the colt was also second in the Woodward Stakes that fall.

During the summer of 1958, Hancock syndicated Nadir into 10 shares, keeping four and the right to stand the colt at Claiborne. The other shareholders were Leonard Sasso, Warner Jones, Howard Keck, Roger Wilson, Daniel Rice, and Fred Hooper.

Although Nadir raced well at four, he did not win another stakes that season, and retired to Claiborne in 1960. His best racer, R. Thomas, came from the stallion's first crop, and Nadir proved to be one of the more disappointing sons of Nasrullah at stud.

The important thing for Claiborne and for Hancock was that horses like Nadir allowed him to play the game: to race at the top level, to attempt to win the classics, and then to have a horse worth putting to stud. In addition to these considerations, Hancock was also trying to find the proper lines for outcrossing with the prominent male lines in the U.S. at that time: especially the lines of Teddy and Fair Play.

Nasrullah fit the bill for an outcross, since there was no other prominent line of Nearco in the country, and Phalaris was represented only through Sickle, Polynesian, Pharamond, and Menow.

In addition to acquiring the Nearco line through Nasrullah, Hancock was able to secure a second line of Nearco through a son of the beautifully formed stallion Royal Charger, who had been imported to stand at Spendthrift Farm, Claiborne's primary rival at the time as a stallion farm.

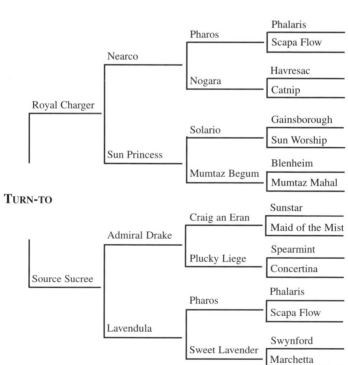

**TURN-TO**

- Royal Charger
  - Nearco
    - Pharos
      - Phalaris
      - Scapa Flow
    - Nogara
      - Havresac
      - Catnip
  - Sun Princess
    - Solario
      - Gainsborough
      - Sun Worship
    - Mumtaz Begum
      - Blenheim
      - Mumtaz Mahal
- Source Sucree
  - Admiral Drake
    - Craig an Eran
      - Sunstar
      - Maid of the Mist
    - Plucky Liege
      - Spearmint
      - Concertina
  - Lavendula
    - Pharos
      - Phalaris
      - Scapa Flow
    - Sweet Lavender
      - Swynford
      - Marchetta

Hancock managed to stand Royal Charger's most successful son, the Garden State Stakes winner Turn-to. Bred in Ireland, the bay was out of the Admiral Drake mare Source Sucree. Claud Tanner had purchased Turn-to as a foal but had died the next year. For Tanner's estate, Hancock consigned the big, handsome bay colt, who sold to Claiborne's client, Harry Guggenheim, for $20,000.

By the time Turn-to was a two-year-old, he had become a highly regarded stakes winner, and both his sire and dam had been imported to the States. Guggenheim had purchased Source Sucree and sent her to Claiborne where he boarded the rest of his mares.

As a juvenile, the colt's best effort prior to winning the Garden State had been in the Saratoga Special, in which he finished second to Porterhouse but got the victory after Porterhouse was disqualified for interference. At the end of his juvenile season, Turn-to was rated equal to Porterhouse at 126 pounds on the Experimental Free Handicap, largely due to his effort in the Garden State Stakes, which occupied a position similar to the Breeders' Cup Juvenile as the richest purse in the country for two-year-old colts.

After the Garden State, Turn-to never lost another race, but he had only three more, all in February of 1954. The next month, the colt bowed a tendon, and he never ran again. Retired to stand at Claiborne, Turn-to had won six of his eight starts, and he was generally believed to have more ability than he had yet shown on the racetracks, as well as more potential for improvement over a distance of ground.

Arthur Hancock recalled his father showing him the horse. "I remember when I was a boy, and my father said, 'I want you to look at this horse. This is the perfect-looking horse, Turn-to.' He came back from the track for a little rest, down there at Barn 20."

Barn 20 is located a good half-mile off the Winchester-Paris Pike. It is a 22-stall barn built at the foot of the hill. An old tobacco barn, Barn 20 was the place used for Claiborne's quarantined horses and layups off the track and was well situated for horses needing therapy on their legs because of a nearby spring. Hancock recalled, "They'd stand Turn-to in that spring, ice-cold water about that deep. It'd cover a horse's knees and everything, and it's still there. And they had it all fenced off and a concrete ramp with notches in it so you wouldn't slip. And Daddy told me, 'This is the perfect horse. Turn-to.' And he said, 'Remember that name.' He was a big horse, as I remember, and a beautiful horse."

Despite prospects never realized, Turn-to became an immediate success as a stallion. His first crop, foals of 1956, included the juvenile champion First Landing (out of the great broodmare Hildene). His third crop held champion Hail to Reason and the fourth, Sir Gaylord.

A half-brother to Horse of the Year Hill Prince, First Landing could hardly have made a more impressive start to his sire's stud career. As a two-year-old, First Landing won 10 of his 11 starts, set a new earnings record for a juvenile, and was champion two-year-old colt of 1958. The next year, First Landing won the Flamingo, ran third in the Kentucky Derby, and continued to win important stakes at four. Although he did not prove to be a major line of transmission for Turn-to's sire line at stud, First Landing did sire Kentucky Derby and Belmont winner Riva Ridge, who retired to stud at Claiborne at the end of 1973.

The major lines of succession came through Sir Gaylord and Hail to Reason. A big and rangy colt who won half of his 18 starts as a two-year-old, Hail to Reason was champion two-year-old colt in 1960. That was also his only season of racing, as the colt injured an ankle in a workout and was retired to stud. Although a juvenile champion, Hail to Reason became an important – even essential – element for stamina in American pedigrees.

In all he sired 42 stakes winners, and Hail to Reason's best included Kentucky Derby winner Proud Clarion, English Derby winner Roberto, Belmont winner Hail to All, Preakness winner Personality, Futurity winner Priceless Gem, as well as champions Straight Deal, Regal Gleam, and Trillion.

Hail to Reason has bred on in the male line principally through his sons Halo and Roberto and through numerous daughters in the bottom lines and internal strains of pedigrees.

Sir Gaylord, like his sire and the champions mentioned above, was a high-class two-year-old. But he shone even brighter in the spring of his third year, winning the Bahamas and Everglades and coming into the

Kentucky Derby as the race favorite for owner-breeder Christopher Chenery. An injury the day before the race ended Sir Gaylord's career, however, and he went to stud at Claiborne. There he sired an even better horse in Sir Ivor, winner of the Grand Criterium at two, the 2,000 Guineas, Derby, and Washington D.C. International at three. Sir Ivor made an important sire standing at Claiborne, getting Arc de Triomphe winner Ivanjica and the leading New Zealand stallion Sir Tristram, among many other outstanding horses.

Sir Gaylord's other top-class racing son and successful stallion was Habitat. A highweighted miler at three, Habitat was the most successful sire standing in Europe during the 1970s and 1980s, getting runners who excelled at distances around a mile.

Although nobody could have realized the extent of his significance in 1960, Turn-to was a stallion who made an exceptional impact on racing and breeding, not just in America but around the world. At the time, however, he was just a very good young stallion getting highly talented racing stock of the sort to make Bull Hancock proud of the decision to stand the horse.

## Loss of Turn-to

The record book shows that the good stallion Turn-to went to stud at Claiborne, and from the first had exceptional success, getting both fast and precocious juveniles, as well as stock that matured well and went two turns.

Such was the response surrounding Turn-to's initial crop that Guggenheim syndicated the stallion into 35 shares priced at $40,000 each, for a total value of $1.4 million. Guggenheim retained 20 shares for his own breeding program. Holding the majority of the shares also allowed him to retain control over the horse.

Then unexpectedly, this exciting young stallion moved from Claiborne to Spendthrift Farm, along with all the other stock owned by the Cain Hoy Stable of Harry Guggenheim. The records do not indicate the reasons for the change.

Maybe the only man now alive who knows, Arthur Hancock said, "I know what happened. It was at night. It was one night about 7:30 when Mr. Guggenheim called Daddy. They didn't have contracts back then for stallions, and Claiborne had four breeding rights, charge for board. And Mr. Guggenheim called about Turn-to after he'd become a good stallion. Mr. Guggenheim told Daddy, 'You can only have three breeding rights this year. I've got to give one of yours to somebody.'

"I can remember him saying on the phone, 'Well, Harry, our agreement is that Claiborne gets four breeding rights. And that's the way it is. That's the way we agreed. That's the way it's gonna be. That's only right.'

"So Mr. Guggenheim kept talking.

"Daddy said, 'Harry, that's the way it's gonna be. Claiborne has four breeding rights. I don't want to discuss the matter any more.' He was getting mad. He had a bad temper, too.

"And then he basically kinda slammed the phone down.

"And then he was really mad, talking ya know."

Hancock had reason to be talking some. Guggenheim had been in racing since the 1930s, and his Cain Hoy Stable had not been famed for success at first. But during the 1950s, with such horses as Kentucky Derby winner Dark Star, Turn-to, and the Nasrullah colt Bald Eagle, Cain Hoy had come up with some top-quality stakes horses. A major contributor to that success had been Bull Hancock.

Arthur Hancock said, "I remember when Mr. Guggenheim came home with Mom and Dad after Dark Star beat Native Dancer (in the 1953 Kentucky Derby). I was a little boy at home, and they came back that night" full of high spirits, bonhomie, and exhilaration.

Now, it was November of 1960, and a blowup was in the works.

Arthur Hancock recalled, "The phone rang right back, pretty quick, and Mr. Guggenheim told Daddy again. He said, 'There's no compromise in this. You're going to get three breedings to Turn-to this coming year.'

Daddy said, 'Harry, have every goddamned horse you've got off this farm tomorrow by sundown, or I'll turn them out on the highway.' And with that, he slammed the phone down. And that was it."

Hancock and Guggenheim parted company permanently. It was a spectacular end to a highly successful relationship, as Guggenheim had used his considerable wealth to acquire excellent stock with Hancock's guidance.

But Arthur Hancock said, "I remember the next day, Van Gorp vans were lined up from the Claiborne office all the way out to the Winchester road. There must have been about 15. Every van they had came in there. They took 20-some yearlings, 30-some mares, the stallions, whatever else was there."

Since Cain Hoy was not a yearling consignor, there was little income lost in that respect, but the loss of the stallions was a major blow, and Turn-to appeared to be the unkindest cut of all. But there was one greater. Among the foals at the time of the change was a colt from the last crop by Nasrullah. The near-black son of Lalun was champion Never Bend, leader of his generation at two and second in the Kentucky Derby at three. Never Bend was also the last top stallion sired by Nasrullah.

Losing the Cain Hoy account "was a huge cost to Claiborne overall," Arthur Hancock said. "But my father had principle. This man was gonna screw him out of one of his breeding rights, and he wouldn't take it. I've always admired that.

"I believe that my father figured that if he was going to do that to him, he'd lost faith in him or something. And it wasn't right. They had an agreement. Dad was a hard worker, and he had other people who respected that and stuck with him, like Mr. Phipps. They didn't have contracts back then. They just had an agreement. Now they've got 30- or 40-page contracts."

The immediate beneficiary of the falling out between Guggenheim and Hancock was Spendthrift Farm. Hancock said, "Of course, they all went to Leslie Combs, and he was like a Cheshire cat."

During his time at Claiborne, Turn-to was an exceptional stallion. With the exception of the good sire Best Turn, all of Turn-to's top sons were sired during his days at Claiborne. Turn-to has proven a very important sire of stallions, and his line continues today. The loss of such a horse would have crushed most operations, psychologically, as well as financially. Unbelievable as it seems, the loss of Turn-to made almost no difference to the success that Claiborne would have in the coming decade.

# Planning and Management

Getting the best bloodstock is only the first step in any breeding program, and it is challenging enough in its own right. David Dink, a well-known statistician and researcher on matters of the Thoroughbred, said that "Bull Hancock was probably even better at selecting stallions than mares. He certainly imported and retained some really good broodmares, but how many other breeders ever put together stallion rosters like his? Nasrullah, Bold Ruler, Princequillo, Round Table, Double Jay, Herbager, Hoist the Flag, Nijinsky, and Forli were all present at the farm within about 10 to 12 years of one another."

The factors that allowed Claiborne to afford to participate in horses of this caliber had been put in order by the elder Hancock, and his son had the discrimination to select many of the best breeding prospects available to him. Claiborne had the financial strength, the reputation for integrity and superior horsemanship, and frankly, the energy of Hancock's personality. These made the farm a magnet for dedicated sportsmen and breeders of substance.

But to breed horses worthy of the farm's reputation and his own high standards, Hancock had to do more than have expensive stallions and wealthy clients. It takes more to breed fast horses consistently.

In my understanding of his process, it began with the smallest details.

In managing stallions, a central issue – that has nothing to do with how successful they are at siring good stock – is keeping them comfortable. This is only good sense. The happier a horse, the easier he is to work with. It makes everything simpler, and there's less chance of endangering a person or a horse.

When Hancock imported Nasrullah, he "had the reputation of being hard horse to handle," Hancock said in an article by Alex Bower in *The Blood-Horse* of Dec. 2, 1950. "He was nervous and excitable and fretful. We turned him out in a paddock where he can see four other stallions. He didn't seem to understand this freedom at first, but he soon adjusted to it, and now he and Double Jay, one of his neighbors, stand across the fence from each other and look like a couple of old cronies."

Getting Nasrullah to relax more in his paddock didn't make the son of Nearco a pussycat. He was still a tough customer. But commonsense horsemanship allowed the horse his space, freedom, and as much company as he wanted.

The Claiborne stallions were given plenty of time to run and graze in their paddocks. The farm also had some of the younger horses ridden, and their diets were adjusted according to the time of year and the amount of exercise they were taking.

In addition to keeping the horses healthy and happy, another serious management concern at Claiborne was the size of a stallion's book. Without the benefit of ultrasound, manual palpation, and other practices common in broodmare management at the end of the 20th century, stallions at the mid-century and earlier covered much smaller books, partly to prevent an oversupply of mares wanting to go to the stallion on the same day.

In the 1950s, the typical book at Claiborne for a young stallion was 20 mares, maybe not even a week's covering for a popular horse today. Double Jay, however, covered 27 mares in his first season, even though he started late: March 19. But Hancock noted in the article above that "he stopped them so well with his first covers that it was not until April 29 – 40 days later – that a mare was returned to him."

Looking after the stallions, having them right and happy, is a small part of the success at Claiborne. It is also one of the sturdy limestone blocks in a foundation that has stood so long and served so well.

CHAPTER TWO

# The Golden Age of Claiborne

The decade of the 1950s was so crucial to the rejuvenation of Claiborne that the events of that time cannot be overemphasized. The rise of Princequillo as a classic sire of national significance, the importation of Nasrullah and other good European stallions as outcrosses to domestic lines, and the buildup of young, quality producers laid out a tremendous path of success for Claiborne as an owner and breeder of top-class racers. But the decade also closed with a seemingly terminal clank, as Nasrullah died in 1959 and Turn-to was moved the following year.

Blows of that sort take a good stallion operation out of the forefront for years, perhaps decades. But Claiborne was anything but average. Bull Hancock's vision for the future went far beyond today and tomorrow. He was planning with a very big picture in mind.

Yet even with that level of pragmatism, the loss of Nasrullah had to make any breeder steady himself and think about what to do next. Without even considering the loss of income from the stallion, Nasrullah meant a great deal to Claiborne and to the Kentucky breeding industry as an emblem of the best qualities and possibilities of the breed.

"Nasrullah was probably as well made a horse as I've ever seen," said Timothy T. Capps, formerly editor of *The Thoroughbred Record* and *Mid Atlantic Thoroughbred*, more recently an executive with the Maryland Jockey Club, and a lifelong lover of the Thoroughbred and its great individuals such as Nasrullah and his son Bold Ruler. "Nasrullah stood about 16.1, so symmetrical, a fabulous mover; he was poetry. I could see how people like Phil Bull and others fell in love with him. He clearly was a horse with tremendous ability."

And as a sire, Nasrullah passed on his outstanding qualities with amazing regularity. Capps believes Nasrullah was able to do this because "he really did put a lot of himself in his stock, and he sired a very typey horse. There was something about the Nasrullahs that was similar. You could see that Nashua and Never Bend had a similarity in balance and top line, although the former was bigger. Nasrullah was clean limbed, not a hint of anything offset."

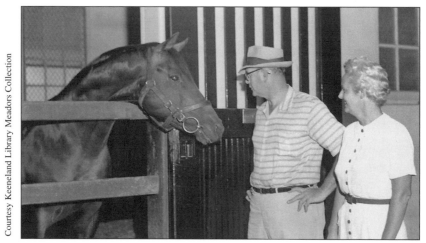

Bull and Waddell Hancock inspect Nasrullah in his stall at Claiborne.

"The Nasrullahs had it all: they were athletic, well-balanced, able to race on any surface. And in my opinion, they had a lot of nerve." Capps recalled that Nasrullah himself "was a tremendous character. He was a really intelligent horse who had a major-league temper. He didn't put on his theatrical show for the people he saw everyday, but when someone came into the shedrow that he didn't recognize, he would put on a show like he was going to tear the barn down."

Nasrullah and his offspring were accustomed to causing a lot of excitement, and in the 1960s, they caused perhaps even more than in the previous decade. Only a handful of the direct offspring of Nasrullah were left to race in that socially and politically turbulent decade, but the sons and daughters of the great stallion took up his legacy and dominated racing and breeding for the next 20 years.

In addition to Nasrullah's influence through the stock he sired that already have received extensive mention, such as Nashua and Delta, and through Never Bend, Fleet Nasrullah, and many other good horses, Nasrullah and his sons became a towering force in the 1960s.

But at the time of the great stallion's death, there was already a stallion at Claiborne, a son of Nasrullah, ready to have an astonishing effect on breeding and racing over the next two decades. His name was Bold Ruler.

"On my first visit to Claiborne," Capps said, "there was a paddock to your right with an old barn up in there. It was a tobacco barn used to hold horses that were off the track or were coming from overseas. In the barn when I visited were Bold Ruler, Court Martial, Nadir, and Nasrina. First time I'd seen Bold Ruler in the flesh."

The recognition of his equine racing hero had a profound effect on Capps, and Bold Ruler, as well as some of his sons, continued to exercise an almost hypnotic power over racing fans and breeders.

In the barn Capps visited in 1958 were three high-class offspring of Nasrullah and the older English stallion Court Martial. Bold Ruler had been Horse of the Year the previous season, Nasrina was named a champion filly in one poll, and Nadir had been a champion two-year-old and a hot prospect for the classics. Nadir had been so highly regarded by Bull Hancock that he rejected several large offers to buy the colt in hopes of winning the Derby with him.

Although the classic plans did work out for Nadir and Claiborne, the year-older Bold Ruler had been a splendid racehorse for Wheatley Stable, one of Claiborne's steadiest and most respected clients. A leading two-year-old and champion at three, Bold Ruler had been a top-class colt every year he raced.

Speaking of his favorite racehorse, Capps admitted that "it's difficult to separate your personal biases and inclinations, but I thought he was a great racehorse in an era of great racehorses. And historically, there is not a greater trio from a single crop than Bold Ruler, Round Table, and Gallant Man. I thought Bold Ruler was the greatest because he was the most versatile, carrying 130-plus pounds as a three-year-old and winning. Then as a four-year-old, he did nothing but carry 130-plus pounds.

**BOLD RULER**

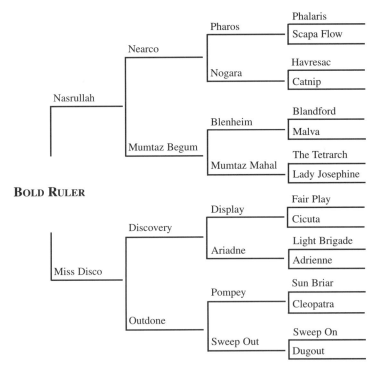

| | | | |
|---|---|---|---|
| | | | Phalaris |
| | | Pharos | Scapa Flow |
| | Nearco | | Havresac |
| | | Nogara | Catnip |
| Nasrullah | | | Blandford |
| | | Blenheim | Malva |
| | Mumtaz Begum | | The Tetrarch |
| | | Mumtaz Mahal | Lady Josephine |
| | | | Fair Play |
| | | Display | Cicuta |
| | Discovery | | Light Brigade |
| | | Ariadne | Adrienne |
| Miss Disco | | | Sun Briar |
| | | Pompey | Cleopatra |
| | Outdone | | Sweep On |
| | | Sweep Out | Dugout |

"He was the best sprinter of his generation, probably the best miler, and could beat the best going 10 furlongs. Plus, he had loads of problems. So arthritic that Dr. Gilman told me that Fitzsimmons would slap Beagle oil on him in the morning, wrap him in blankets, and then walk him around until he was really loose."

When Bold Ruler was a racehorse, the story tended to focus on which of his physical troubles was nagging him at the time. Some soreness with his mouth was mentioned as the reason for the fast bay's headstrong behavior in the Kentucky Derby, when he ran fourth, and a change of bit and some of Sunny Jim Fitzsimmons' magic enabled Bold Ruler to relax better in the Preakness and scoot home to victory.

The previous season, Bold Ruler had been the country's leading juvenile until a pair of losses late in the year, especially a loss in the all-important Garden State Stakes, handed the championship to Garden State Stakes winner Barbizon, who was owned by Calumet Farm. Soreness in Bold Ruler's back and hindquarters seemed to be the culprit in that case. But the good-sized bay son of Nasrullah had been dogged by trouble from the first. Hancock said that Bold Ruler was a very skinny foal with a large hernia when he was quite young. The colt outgrew this but developed a tendency to walk his stall. Hancock claimed that he was never thoroughly pleased with Bold Ruler's condition while he was growing up at Claiborne but noted that he had a good disposition and never missed an oat.

Hancock would have had some experience with the offspring of Bold Ruler's dam, Miss Disco. The Discovery mare lived at Claiborne and was a regular mate for Nasrullah. Bold Ruler was the third foal by Nasrullah out of Miss Disco. In all she produced six foals by the stallion, three colts and three fillies. All three of the colts were stakes winners, and the best of the fillies was stakes-placed Eastern Princess.

Winner of the Futurity at two and nearly champion at that age, Bold Ruler improved greatly at three. He ran some tremendous races against Gen. Duke during the first part of 1957, winning the Flamingo and losing the Florida Derby in record time. In his final prep for the Kentucky Derby, Bold Ruler won the Wood Memorial over Gallant Man and then was fourth as the favorite in the Derby.

He bounced back to win the Preakness. Despite a couple more losses, further victories in the Jerome, the Vosburgh, and then especially in the Trenton Handicap against his principal rivals Round Table and Gallant Man (winner of the Belmont) sent the divisional honors and the Horse of the Year title to Bold Ruler.

After five major handicap victories at four, as well as a game loss in the Metropolitan Handicap, Bold Ruler was retired to stud with 23 victories in 33 starts and more than three-quarters of a million dollars in earnings.

"He was a great stallion from the first," Capps said. "They went two turns, despite popular opinion to the contrary. It was bad luck, in my opinion, that he didn't get a Triple Crown horse until Secretariat."

Standing his first season in 1959, Bold Ruler's first foals were born in 1960, the year his sire's last crop hit the ground. Bold Ruler became the country's leading sire for the first time in 1963, when his oldest foals were only three. His best racer that year was champion filly Lamb Chop, who was rather lightly made and elegant, along the lines of her broodmare sire Count Fleet.

In 1964, Bold Ruler's champions were Bold Lad and Queen Empress, so that the stallion swept both divisions of the juvenile rankings. Bold Ruler later sired the champion two-year-old colts Successor (a full brother to Bold Lad) and Vitriolic, as well as the champion juvenile filly Queen of the Stage. During this blush of success, Bold Ruler led the general sire list seven times: from 1963 through 1969, and gained an eighth general sire title in 1973 when Secretariat won the Triple Crown.

With statistics like that, it is no wonder that Capps said, "Bold Ruler was the best stallion in the world. To an uncommon degree, his stud career mirrored his racing career." For all his success, Bold Ruler was criticized by some commentators as only a sire of speed horses and good two-year-olds. Among the evidence used to justify these opinions, Bold Lad and his full brother, Successor, tended to get a good deal of blame from the knockers of their sire. It is true that both were high-class racers as two-year-olds, and neither was quite as dominant later as he had been at two, although in Bold Lad's case, it wasn't for lack of ability or willingness. He just had a hard time staying sound.

As handsome a horse as you might find, unless you were looking at Secretariat, Bold Lad was fairly typical of one type of the Bold Ruler stock. They were quite handsome, even flashy, and gifted with speed and great power.

A very fluent mover on the racetrack, Bold Lad is generally credited as being the most athletically talented son of Bold Ruler, aside from Secretariat. In his juvenile season, Bold Lad won the Hopeful and Futurity in very fast times, then crushed his opposition in the Champagne. The handsome chestnut closed his juvenile career with eight victories in 10 starts.

He skipped the Garden State Stakes and Pimlico Futurity because trainer Bill Winfrey wanted to give Bold Lad plenty of time to grow and become sounder. In *The Blood-Horse* of Oct. 24, 1964, Winfrey explained that the champion colt had trouble with his right knee. He said, "To the hand, it's not as flat as the other one. It's a little warm – not hot, but not as cool as the other one."

Winfrey prescribed time and a couple of blisters. Unfortunately, Bold Lad popped a splint on his right foreleg in February of 1965, was delayed further in his training and racing, turned in a dull performance in New York, but then won the Derby Trial in his belated final prep for the Derby that year.

The understudies to Bold Lad for the 1965 classics in the Phippses' stable were Dapper Dan, owned by Ogden Phipps, and Wheatley's Bold Bidder. Dapper Dan, a stretch-running son of Ribot, picked up seconds in the Kentucky Derby and Preakness.

Bold Lad ran in the Derby and started favorite but was horribly beaten. In July, he had chips taken out of his offending right knee and did not run again until 1966.

In a brief campaign at four, Bold Lad again showed that he was an immensely talented racer. Trained at four by Eddie Neloy, Bold Lad won the Roseben Handicap and then the Metropolitan under 132 pounds.

Although full brothers, Bold Lad and Successor were very different kinds of racehorses. Bold Lad was full of speed and light. Successor was bay, more lightly made, and more like his dam, the champion racemare Misty Morn.

Even so, Successor was a Bold Ruler, and he came to hand six months to a year earlier than Misty Morn, a daughter of Princequillo and the great broodmare Grey Flight. Successor won his first stakes, the Tremont, in July at Aqueduct. But the bay colt won his championship in October and November with victories in the Champagne and the Garden State Stakes. In the Champagne, he defeated the previously unbeaten Dr. Fager.

Essentially, Successor was a staying two-year-old, rather than a powerful colt with quick and explosive speed like Bold Lad. Such differing qualities are not unusual, even in full brothers, and the different expression of the same gene pool indicates the challenges that breeders of the Thoroughbred face as they work up matings and hope for the best.

In the case of breeding Bold Ruler to Misty Morn, the best is what Wheatley Stable routinely produced. Successor was the fifth stakes winner from his dam. As his dam's successor more than his sire's, Successor trained on as a distance-loving and rather one-paced colt at three, winning the Lawrence Realization and finishing third in the Jockey Club Gold Cup.

Whereas Successor stood a fraction under 16 hands at the end of his two-year-old season, many other sons and daughters of Bold Ruler were more substantial, even imposing. Champion Vitriolic was "well above 16 hands at the wither and even higher than that at the croup," according to *Daily Racing Form's* Charlie Hatton.

Out of the Ambiorix mare Sarcastic, Vitriolic was champion colt of 1967, and Bold Ruler's daughter Queen of the Stage took honors as the leading juvenile filly that season. She, too, stood more than 16 hands at two but was generally more refined than Vitriolic.

The same year, Gamely was champion three-year-old filly according to the Thoroughbred Racing Association handicappers in a division in which the voting groups split their awards, with the *Racing Form* selecting Furl Sail. Winner of the Alabama, Gamely was yet another example of a Bold Ruler who won at the highest level going 10 furlongs or more.

In this regard, she joined Bold Bidder, Bold Hour, and Lamb Chop, and the next question is how many sires ever get a horse possessing this level of ability? Obviously very few do. But Bold Ruler was criticized due to the minority of his stakes winners' winning at longer distances. The observers' notion that the Bold Rulers did not stay 10 furlongs came initially, I believe, from the fact that there were so many good horses by Bold Ruler, and most stakes races in this country, except for a handful of championship level events, are at distances of a mile or less. Then the case regarding stamina in Bold Ruler's progeny was complicated further by a few extremely talented and high-profile horses, notably Bold Lad, who did not win at 10 furlongs.

Gamely, however, could do just about anything. She set a track record in winning the Test Stakes at Saratoga, then won the Alabama at a mile and a quarter. She had speed, and she carried it. Although unraced at two, Gamely developed into a top filly at three, then improved at four and five.

Rarely has a mare been better named, as Gamely carried the fight to her competition time and again. Champion older mare at four, Gamely was probably the best daughter of Bold Ruler. Unlike Vitriolic, she was not exceptionally tall, only 16 hands, but "with the scope and substance to match," in the words of Charlie Hatton. He described her as "a claybank bay with a large star and snip and white fetlocks behind." But in addition to the nerve of a champion, the parts of her makeup that made Gamely a top racer were strength and proportion. Hatton noted that "she has Bold Ruler's evident power about the hindquarters. Gamely is a trifle wide in the front fork, with an immense, round barrel and no suggestion of weakness rises from her flanks, for all the length of her middle. She is extremely wide across the loin and hips. Her quarters, viewed from the side, form an elongated bow which extends well down toward the hock."

Bull Hancock and William Haggin Perry bred Gamely in partnership, although she ran in Perry's colors. The mare was such a favorite with Perry that he eventually named his operation the Gamely Corp. The arrangement with Perry grew out of Hancock's continuing desire to generate cash flow on some of the Claiborne stock and still retain horses for racing and breeding.

In the arrangement with Perry, Hancock would sell a half-interest in the entire crop, then pair the yearlings up, with each partner selecting which one he would like to race. After the first round of purchases, the horses selected for retirement to Claiborne and for breeding another generation were sent home as partnership stock. Horses bred by the partners were divided up as yearlings, sent into training by each operation, then after retirement put back into the partnership. This gave each man the opportunity to race horses in his own name, yet offered some individuality and independence in goals and inclinations.

The My Babu mare Gambetta was the dam of Gamely and came into this partnership after Hancock had purchased Gambetta and her dam Rough Shod in 1961. Thomas Girdler, president of Republic Steel, had imported Rough Shod into the U.S. and sent her to Claiborne in late 1951. At the time, Rough Shod was carrying Gambetta.

A decade later, the mares had been useful for Girdler, but in a telephone discussion with Hancock one morning, Girdler declared that he wanted to sell both mares, as well as Rough Shod's short two-year-old by Nantallah. Hancock was later quoted as telling "Mr. Girdler he shouldn't sell them, but he insisted, said he was getting too old."

The outcome was that Moody Jolley purchased the colt and named him Ridan. Hancock himself purchased both Rough Shod and Gambetta. Not long thereafter, Rough Shod foaled Lt. Stevens as one of her five foals for Claiborne.

"Rough Shod was well named – big and on the coarse side," Capps said. "But I kinda like those types of mares because there is a toughness, almost a masculine trait, to them. When you when find one, you can breed them to any stallion and take a chance on refining those qualities. She tended to get a type that was more like herself, but in what Claiborne bred her to, they were trying to get a little more refined individual." Not a mare who possessed a summer sale pedigree, Rough Shod had such an illustrious producing career that her daughters did become summer sale mares and some of the most desirable producers in the world.

Although she was carrying Gambetta at the time of Girdler's purchase, Rough Shod really wasn't an immediate success. Only just before she came into the Claiborne broodmare band did she really strike the right balance at stud.

It came in her first mating with Nantallah, and the bright bay colt they produced was bred by Girdler and named Ridan. After winning his first few starts at two, John Greer, a Memphis bakery company owner and a Claiborne client, and Ernest Woods bought interests in Ridan from Jolley, and the partners raced the colt through the rest of his career. A grand-looking colt and a very fast one, the success of the mating confirmed Hancock in believing that the mare should return to Nantallah.

In volume, Claiborne did less well with Gambetta, as she produced only three foals for the farm. But there was a star in the trio. A stakes-winning two-year-old, Gambetta was a solid producer from the beginning, but when mated to Bold Ruler, she bloomed her best rose in Gamely.

Such was the success of Rough Shod and her descendants in the coming years that Claiborne became identified with Rough Shod, and her offspring have produced many of the farm's elemental contributions to the breed.

At the time he bought her from Girdler, Rough Shod was another good mare that Hancock acquired for the farm's use without any reason to expect what wonders lay ahead. It was a simple decision, and Hancock was quoted in *Daily Racing Form* saying that he purchased Rough Shod because he "liked her family. It is one of those strong, old Irish families."

A big, strong mare that some would even describe as rough, Rough Shod was an outstanding producer, getting champion Moccasin for Claiborne to the cover of the Nasrullah stallion Nantallah. Rough Shod produced the very best offspring by that relatively minor son of Nasrullah, and some pedigree commentators would say that she was the only reason Nantallah is memorable today.

That is going too far, however. Rough Shod fit Nantallah very well, and "Bull paid a lot of attention to physical type," Capps noted. "In addition to looking at pedigree and race record and quality, he was always looking for the proper physical types to match well with the different programs of the Claiborne clients." So there is just the significant possibility that we would not have heard so much about Rough Shod if

Hancock hadn't mated her to Nantallah. It was a match that worked. Rough Shod produced two stakes-winning colts, with Ridan being her best son.

Of her daughters, Rough Shod's best was Moccasin, a champion two-year-old and full sister to Ridan, who had started favorite in the 1962 Kentucky Derby but finished third. Moccasin was bred by Claiborne, and Hancock's initial worry about her was that "she might get too big for us," as quoted in *The Thoroughbred Record* early in 1966. Sent to trainer Harry Trotsek as a yearling in late 1964, Moccasin was big and gangly. Nothing serious was asked of her early, but the first time Trotsek let her breeze, she was exceptional and moved without effort. In the same article mentioned above, Trotsek said, "We knew we could have started her in January or February in those baby races, and she would have won." That alone is an indication of the natural athleticism of a filly who was otherwise big, growthy, and appearing to need time.

Rather than using her to win some races of minor significance, however, Hancock wanted this filly for the long haul and elected to wait. Moccasin repaid his patience with victories in the Spinaway, Matron, Alcibiades, Selima, and Gardenia, going undefeated at two and seemingly untested. She had defeated her contemporaries in the juvenile fillies division with ease, and the exceptionally well-grown Hail to Reason filly Priceless Gem had beaten Buckpasser in the Futurity. So through that line of form, Moccasin was considered in some parts the superior of the Phipps champion colt of 1965.

As the standout champion of her sex at two and Horse of the Year in some polls, Moccasin at one point appeared a threat to outdo her older brother Ridan. And she was for a time pointed to the Kentucky Derby. That did not work out, as she did not retain her form and level of superiority over other fillies as she matured from two to three.

In fact, both champion juveniles of 1965, Moccasin and Buckpasser, didn't have much going their way in the first half of 1966. Buckpasser had been knocked out of competition for the Triple Crown due to a quarter crack early in the year.

The best horse raised at Claiborne during the 1960s, Buckpasser was bred and raced by Ogden Phipps, and aside from his excellence and great physical quality, Buckpasser also is notable for being the best Phipps horse of the decade with no Bold Ruler blood.

By Horse of the Year Tom Fool out of the War Admiral mare Busanda, Buckpasser won 12 of his 13 starts at three, was named champion three-year-old colt and Horse of the Year, then the following year joined his sire and dam as a winner of the Suburban Handicap.

A colt who began his second season looking angular and almost too refined, Buckpasser grew and strengthened throughout. After his quarter crack had grown out, he returned to racing on the Belmont Stakes card, running six furlongs in 1:09 1/5. In the main event, Kentucky Derby and Preakness winner Kauai King was shuffled into fourth after nearly racing away with Buckpasser's Triple Crown.

Trained by Eddie Neloy like many of the other Phipps champions, Buckpasser set a record for the mile in the Arlington Classic, surpassed $1 million in earnings with victory in the Travers, and completely humiliated his older competition with victories in the Brooklyn Handicap, Woodward, and Jockey Club Gold Cup.

Although many high-class horses receive more praise than good judgment would dictate as reasonable, in the case of Buckpasser, it is challenging to praise the horse more than he deserves. Perhaps it is easier to define him by what he was not. Not a sprinter nor a headstrong frontrunner, neither a very interested work horse in the mornings nor a racer who generally seemed to think of the early furlongs in a race as much more than a curiosity to observe,

Buckpasser was the ultimate heart attack horse.

While he had worlds of speed, Buckpasser liked to dole it out in bits and dabs. With a seemingly catatonic Braulio Baeza riding him, Buckpasser might lag near the end of a race or lie quietly in mid-pack until the stretch. Then, the horse's formidable finishing power and gameness would bring him to the front.

Nobody who has seen Buckpasser's finish in the 1967 Suburban, when he seemed to be hopelessly beaten but swept to victory in the last stride, can do aught but marvel at the horse's native ability and

**BUCKPASSER**

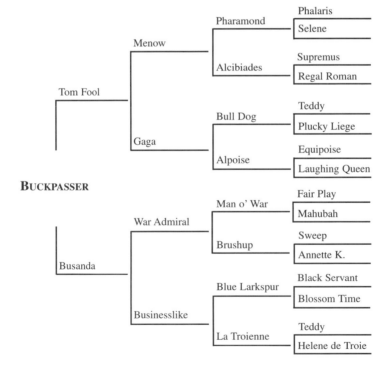

| | | | Phalaris |
| | | Pharamond | |
| | Menow | | Selene |
| | | | Supremus |
| Tom Fool | | Alcibiades | |
| | | | Regal Roman |
| | | | Teddy |
| | | Bull Dog | |
| | Gaga | | Plucky Liege |
| | | | Equipoise |
| | | Alpoise | |
| | | | Laughing Queen |
| | | | Fair Play |
| | | Man o' War | |
| | War Admiral | | Mahubah |
| | | | Sweep |
| Busanda | | Brushup | |
| | | | Annette K. |
| | | | Black Servant |
| | | Blue Larkspur | |
| | Businesslike | | Blossom Time |
| | | | Teddy |
| | | La Troienne | |
| | | | Helene de Troie |

66

perhaps his quirky intelligence that allowed him to accomplish so much with so little fanfare.

Having won 25 races from 31 starts and nearly $1.5 million, Buckpasser was retired to stud at the end of 1967 to his birthplace, Claiborne Farm. A good-sized horse of great quality, Buckpasser stood more than 16.2 hands as a three-year-old, and he filled in when he matured as a stallion.

In type, Buckpasser was notably rangier and scopier than his sire Tom Fool, a true powerhouse who had tremendous depth through the shoulder and strength across his hips. Tom Fool tended to sire horses who ran a mile very well, and some stayed classic distances. Buckpasser, as one of the most emphatic of these, also showed his great resemblance to the qualities of his dam, Alabama and Suburban winner Busanda, and to her sire, Triple Crown winner War Admiral.

And as he went to stud at Claiborne, there was an inevitable inclination to see him both as the successor to Bold Ruler and the natural outcross to provide stamina and quality to the strong, fast Bold Ruler broodmares.

## The Search for the Outcross

Since Bold Ruler was the leading sire in North America seven years in a row during the 1960s, he made an indelible mark upon Claiborne. He even went a long way toward defining the farm during that time. But he was far from the only top-class sire at the farm. In fact, Claiborne stallions led the national sire list for 15 consecutive years through the 1950s and 1960s. So Bold Ruler wasn't all of the story. But together with his sire, Nasrullah, they were responsible for a dozen of those leading sire laurels, with Princequillo taking three sire titles and Ambiorix getting one.

"I wouldn't argue that Bold Ruler created the American type of horse, since his own sire had a major role in that," Capps said, "but he helped to establish a type of horse that breeders wanted: Fast two-year-olds who trained on and became top three-year-olds."

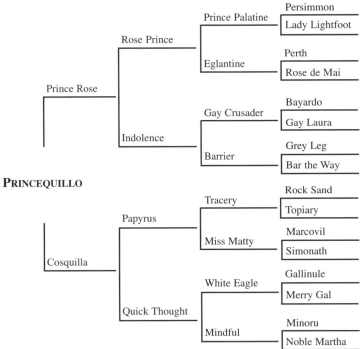

**PRINCEQUILLO**

| | | | |
|---|---|---|---|
| | | | Persimmon |
| | | Prince Palatine | Lady Lightfoot |
| | Rose Prince | | Perth |
| | | Eglantine | Rose de Mai |
| Prince Rose | | | Bayardo |
| | | Gay Crusader | Gay Laura |
| | Indolence | | Grey Leg |
| | | Barrier | Bar the Way |
| | | | Rock Sand |
| | | Tracery | Topiary |
| | Papyrus | | Marcovil |
| | | Miss Matty | Simonath |
| Cosquilla | | | Gallinule |
| | | White Eagle | Merry Gal |
| | Quick Thought | | Minoru |
| | | Mindful | Noble Martha |

And just as he had been when Nasrullah was the top stallion in the preceding decade, Bull Hancock was looking for the proper outcross, trying to balance the speed and early maturity with the scope and toughness to compete in the classics.

To this end, Hancock already had the best outcross sire in the country, and his name was Princequillo. Born the same year as Nasrullah (1940), Princequillo was a bay son of Prince Rose and the Papyrus mare Cosquilla and was bred in England, brought to race in the U.S. during World War II. Horatio Luro claimed Princequillo for $2,500 as a two-year-old for Boone Hall Stable and developed the colt into a top-class stayer at three and four, when he won the Saratoga Cup and Jockey Club Gold Cup, along with other good races.

After two seasons at Ellerslie in Virginia, Princequillo was moved to Claiborne. In his second season at stud in Virginia, Princequillo had sired a bay colt for Christopher Chenery later named Hill Prince. That colt was a top-class two-year-old who became Horse of the Year at three. Other champions by Princequillo include Misty Morn, Dedicate, Quill, and Round Table.

All three of Princequillo's champion sons went to stud at Claiborne. Hill Prince sired champion Bayou out of Claiborne mare Bourtai, Dedicate sired champion Smart Deb, and Round Table became one of the best stallions in the world.

Princequillo's daughters, to an even greater degree than his sons, became an essential part of breeding and racing. Bold Ruler sired a pair of champion colts from Misty Morn in Bold Lad and Successor, along with numerous stakes winners out of other daughters of Princequillo. And Bold Ruler's best son came from the Princequillo mare Somethingroyal.

Hancock, however, was not a man who sat around waiting for success to come to him. Continually searching for more good horses, he added a wide international cross-section of outcross stallions to the Claiborne lineup through the 1960s.

The two most immediately successful of these new horses were the French-bred classic winner Herbager and the Argentine-bred classic winner Forli. Others included Pronto, Sky High, and Le Fabuleux.

The last-named horse was a very big, impressive chestnut. In many ways, Le Fabuleux was greatly different from the type of horses that Hancock had built his greatest successes upon.

The dominant type of stallion that Hancock selected in the 1950s was the medium-sized, beautifully balanced, high-quality horses best seen in Nasrullah, Princequillo, Ambiorix, and Double Jay. Although those horses had differing levels of success, along with somewhat different aptitudes, each had speed, maneuverability, and versatility. Even though Princequillo, for instance, did not have great success on the track until racing classic distances, he was so well made that he was consistently able to sire stock that proved effective at distances around a mile.

In contrast, Herbager and Le Fabuleux were considerably atypical from the earlier pattern, but they were good sires, especially Herbager, and they also were good broodmare sires. Taking the long-term view was clearly part of Hancock's plan.

In looking at the pedigrees and lines he developed over the years, Hancock's long-term plans and goals surely included blending the quick American lines with a core of middle-distance horses to produce racing stock that would be a force at Claiborne and in American breeding for years to come.

On the surface of things, Le Fabuleux was the antithesis of an American type of stallion. He was really big, somewhat temperamental, and straight in his pasterns, but he still managed to be a good stallion at Claiborne. As his French pedigree and race record indicated, Le Fabuleux was a stallion who was completely classic. As a sire, he was simply not going to get early-maturing racehorses who won the big races at six furlongs. Ever.

But I don't believe that was even a consideration in Hancock's mind. Judging from what he did, the goal of producing the supreme racehorse was synonymous with producing the classic racehorse.

And, due to the number of fast horses and early-maturing horses already available to Claiborne and its clients, Hancock felt secure enough to add these relatively risky and atypical stallions to the lineup at the farm. In the long-term, he succeeded with them, too.

The most successful Kentucky Derby winner of the 1990s after he went to stud in Kentucky, for instance, was Unbridled. A really big horse out of a lovely mare by Le Fabuleux, Unbridled blended the speed of Raise a Native, Dr. Fager, and Mr. Prospector with the size, strength, and constitution of Le Fabuleux to become a truly classic racehorse and sire, spending the latter years of his stud career at Claiborne.

In addition to acquiring a pair of French Derby winners in Le Fabuleux and Herbager, as well as high-class racers from the Southern Hemisphere, Hancock also secured a pair of home-grown stallion prospects in the mid-1960s who provided outcross potential, were commercially mainstream, more obviously the Claiborne type, and who proved to be outstanding sires. They were foaled in consecutive years, as Buckpasser was a foal of 1963, Damascus a foal of 1964. Buckpasser was retired to stud a year earlier than his younger rival, who defeated him for Horse of the Year with a wide-margin success in the 1967 Woodward Stakes, although Buckpasser was past his best form at that point.

When Ogden Phipps syndicated Buckpasser for stud, the owner-breeder retained a half-interest in the horse and sold the 16 other shares in the 32-share syndicate for $150,000 each, giving the horse a total valuation of $4.8 million, although only $2.4 million in equity was actually sold. Since the Phipps family had a decades-long relationship with the Hancock family, it was almost as natural as maple leaves turning color in the fall that Buckpasser went to stud at Claiborne.

Furthermore, Hancock and Ogden Phipps were great friends, as well as devoted lovers of the Thoroughbred. Seth Hancock recalled that his father "talked to Mr. Phipps a lot at night, but he never talked to us about what went on with the farm."

When Bull Hancock came home from his day on the farm, he was ready for family life, not business, except for his friendly conversations with Phipps. Seth Hancock said, "They'd have a 15-20 minute conversation most nights. Mr. Phipps didn't have a lot of friends, but he loved the horses. And he loved to talk about it. He'd probably have him a drink at night, and he'd want to talk to somebody. And of course Daddy had the horses here and loved Mr. Phipps like we all did."

As a result of their common interests and their conversations over the years, Hancock and Phipps became very close friends. Relatively unknown as an individual to the press and general public, Phipps was one of the most significant breeders of the 20th century, and he kept his horses at Claiborne Farm, where the Hancock family has raised Phipps-bred horses for three generations.

Seth Hancock noted that one of the reasons people knew so little about Phipps personally was that although Phipps "was a wonderful guy, he was tremendously shy. And everybody took that for him being aloof and stuck-up. Nothing could be further from the truth. Nicest guy you'd ever be around or know, and absolutely loved the horses. Just a great man."

A serious and very successful breeder, Phipps "had some tremendous luck, but there was probably a lot more to it than luck," Hancock said, "and I'm not talking about Claiborne's part, either. I'm talking about the accomplishments on his part. It was something he thought about all the time. He spent the whole month at Saratoga. He'd watch which stallions were coming along, were having runners and not having runners. He was always on the lookout to try to buy a nice mare if you saw one, so he was freshening up all the time. He put a lot into the game. So he deserved to get a lot out of it. And he did."

In those flush days of the 1960s, the Phippses were conquering the world of racing with such regularity that Buckpasser as a two-year-old seemed just another Phipps champion. As it turned out, he was the best horse Ogden Phipps ever raced, and after the bay son of Tom Fool had sped through his three-year-old season, he had won 12 of his 13 starts in his second season and had lost only two races to that point in his career. After some disappointments at four, Buckpasser was retired to Claiborne amid far-reaching hopes and plans.

As Wheatley Stable had retained full ownership in Bold Ruler and had greatly profited from complete control of the stallion, there was likely a feeling that retaining a larger portion of Buckpasser would be the best path to follow.

Whereas Wheatley had kept Bold Ruler as something close to a private stallion, Buckpasser was half-syndicated and open to the market's influence to that extent. With Bold Ruler, seasons were available to breeders under a special arrangement. The breeder would nominate two mares and, if selected, could breed both of them to Bold Ruler with the understanding that Wheatley would get one foal and the breeder would get the other. Return matings of top-class mares allowed the Phipps racing stable practically to bulge with an overloading of top prospects that had exotic pedigrees.

This policy kept the number of Bold Ruler's offspring available for sale at the yearling auctions to an unbelievable minimum by contemporary standards. In contrast, opening up Buckpasser's book to the marketplace was a somewhat more modern approach. But Phipps did retain half the horse, clearly with a view to maximizing Buckpasser's potential influence on his own racing operation.

Going into the 1968 breeding season, there had to be a sense of elation and expectancy that Buckpasser would be a tremendous match for Bold Ruler mares and would provide the Phippses with the classic racers they had looked for in their breeding and racing program, much like Hancock himself.

With the goal of the classics in mind, and especially with regard to providing a successful outcross or nick with Bold Ruler, Buckpasser was a tremendous disappointment.

To the contrary, the cross between the two stallions proved to be a classic anti-nick. The only top-class runner bred on the cross was a filly named Quick as Lightning. Bred by the Phippses and raced in England, she was a high-class juvenile filly who won the 1,000 Guineas at Newmarket at three. Quick as Lightning was out of the Bold Ruler mare Clear Ceiling, a full sister to leading sire What a Pleasure and a half-sister to the champion and outstanding producer Misty Morn. The dam of all three was the great broodmare Grey Flight.

But Quick as Lightning came very late in Buckpasser's stud career, and he had done very good work earlier. From his first crop, the champion two-year-old Buckpasser sired a champion two-year-old filly in Numbered Account.

The stallion's second crop contained his second champion two-year-old filly in La Prevoyante, who won a dozen races without defeat as a juvenile, and a couple of heretics even mentioned her as possibly being superior to her contemporary Secretariat.

Numbered Account and La Prevoyante were similar in type, quality, and racing class. They also set the stage for Buckpasser's lasting influence through his daughters. Although Numbered Account continued to have a successful career and became an important broodmare after her retirement to stud at Claiborne, La Prevoyante died before being put to stud, as did Quick as Lightning.

Their loss seems an even sadder injustice in hindsight, given the quality of Buckpasser's daughters as producers.

Despite Buckpasser's excellence as a producer of race fillies and broodmares, his colts were quite good, too. Some of them even went on to have a measure of success as stallions. With Silver Buck (winner of the Suburban and Whitney) being his most successful son and siring Kentucky Derby winner Silver Charm, Buckpasser also had the useful sires Buckaroo (Kentucky Derby winner Spend a Buck), State Dinner (champion Family Style), L'Enjoleur (Groovy), and Buckfinder (Track Barron).

Several of Buckpasser's sons also showed better success as broodmare sires than as sires of stakes winners.

In comparison to Buckpasser, Damascus was not quite so exceptionally pedigreed, but he was a first-class racehorse. Although not a genuine speedball as a juvenile, Damascus came to his best form late at two, then continued his improvement at three to win both the Preakness and Belmont Stakes. A convincing winner against his own age group and his elders later in his three-year-old season, Damascus was Horse of the Year in 1967. Like Buckpasser, he found his four-year-old season highly competitive, swapping victories with the great Dr. Fager, who took honors as Horse of the Year in 1968.

Retired to stud at Claiborne, Damascus had shown speed and toughness. As a sire, he showed that he could get quick juveniles with some versatility, and many of his progeny matured well, as their sire had done. He did not come out with a champion like Numbered Account or La Prevoyante in his first crops. But he did get quality stakes winners. They showed speed. Some of his stock reached their form early, others late. Although he sired a few sprinters, most of the racers by Damascus carried their speed at least a mile, and some were very well suited to the classics.

The most classic sons by Damascus included Highland Blade, who ran second in the Belmont and won the Marlboro Cup and Brooklyn at five; Diabolo, a classy two-year-old who ran third in the Kentucky Derby and Preakness; and Desert Wine, second in the Kentucky Derby. Other sons of note included Ogygian, winner of the Futurity at two and a good sire at Claiborne before his export to Japan; Judger, winner of the Blue Grass Stakes and a useful sire at Claiborne; and Bailjumper, winner of the Dwyer whose best son was Skip Trial, a Grade 1 winner at three, four, and five whose best son is Horse of the Year Skip Away.

Far and away, however, the most influential second-generation influence by Damascus has been Private Account, out of Buckpasser's champion daughter Numbered Account. Clearly struck from the Buckpasser mold with quality and scope, Private Account also inherited strength and power from Damascus. Both elements were helpful to the stallion's success, as he made the most of his opportunities at Claiborne, siring horses with reasonable speed and considerable stamina, horses capable of performing well at two and maturing into top-flight performers, and horses with the capacity to race well on turf and on dirt courses across the world.

Of his many fine performers, none was equal to the unbeaten champion Personal Ensign. A winner at Grade 1 level at two, three, and four, Personal Ensign won each of her 13 starts, closing her career with a tremendous effort to succeed in the Breeders' Cup Distaff. Favored against Kentucky Derby winner Winning Colors, Personal Ensign seemed hopelessly beaten as the field turned into the stretch. But under a leaden sky on a cold and dreary day, Personal Ensign was not to be denied. She lit up the afternoon with a bloom of light as she closed relentlessly, taking the lead almost at the wire.

Among Private Account's other top runners are Personal Flag, a full brother to Personal Ensign and the stallion's most accomplished son at stud, Chimes of Freedom, and East of the Moon, winner of the Poule d'Essai des Pouliches and Prix de Diane.

And in keeping with his similarities to Buckpasser, Private Account has become an important sire of quality broodmares. Chimes of Freedom, for instance, has produced four stakes winners already, including champion Aldebaran, by Mr. Prospector.

As the potential outcross lines and prospective nicks for Bold Ruler and the eminent Claiborne lines were being acquired, Bold Ruler's own sons also were taking their places at stud. The early returns from these sons were not bad, but the more intent focus of critically observant breeders was on the first son that owners and breeders thought might become a rival or at least a significant continuation of Bold Ruler's line: Bold Lad.

He was so handsome. He was so fast. He was so talented. He was so not sound. And that, unfortunately, pretty much tells the tale of Bold Lad as a sire. When the first few crops, after showing speed and promise, failed to carry through with top-class performances, Bold Lad was sent to France in 1972, and from there he was exported to Japan in 1978, where he died in 1986.

Although not a smasher on his European tour, among his stock raced overseas, Bold Lad sired Sirlad, Bold Fascinator, Gentle Thoughts, and Marble Arch, all highweights in one major European racing venue or another. Among his American-raced offspring, Rube the Great (Wood Memorial, Gotham) was the best.

Another Bold Ruler colt raised at Claiborne provided the first indications of how grand and how classically oriented Bold Ruler's influence would be throughout the coming decade.

Big and growthy but with high ability, Bold Bidder, bred and initially raced by Wheatley Stable, was sold to Paul Falkenstein midway through his three-year-old season. A good winner who had set the pace in the 1965 Belmont Stakes, Bold Bidder improved immensely toward the end of the year. John Gaines leased the bay colt in November of 1965 with an option to purchase and raced him to victories in the 1966 Strub Stakes, Monmouth Handicap, and Hawthorne Gold Cup. Gaines, in partnership with John Olin and John Hanes, exercised his option, purchased Bold Bidder outright, and retired him to stud at Gainesway Farm in 1967.

Unraced at two and a rather atypical Bold Ruler in that regard, Bold Bidder was tough and became sounder as he matured. He also proved to be one of the two or three best stallions by Bold Ruler, getting a pair of Kentucky Derby winners in Cannonade and Spectacular Bid.

The successes of Bold Bidder in races like the Strub, along with the efforts of Secretariat and Wajima at 10 furlongs and beyond, did much to erase the bias that Bold Rulers did not stay a distance. But like many biases, it outlasted any opportunity to apply a different constructive approach.

In July of 1970, Bold Ruler began showing signs of labored breathing, and further examination showed that he had a tumor just below his brain, situated near the junction of the nasal passage and the throat. After surgery and radiation to destroy the tumor, the stallion was expected to have a normal life span. That did not prove to be the case.

The following year, the cancer recurred, and Bold Ruler was put down on July 12, 1971. His greatest son, Secretariat, was a yearling, and the stallion's final crop, which included champion Wajima, was born in 1972.

As great a stallion as he unquestionably was, a cardinal quality that stands out about Bold Ruler is the consistently high ability of his progeny. From 356 foals, he sired 82 stakes winners for 23 percent stakes winners to foals. That percentage is amazingly large and is a tribute both to the horse's value as a sire and to Claiborne's success in managing him. Overall, nearly half of Bold Ruler's named foals were black-type quality horses.

Perhaps the only blemish on the stallion's record is that although several of his sons were quite good and a few of them even led the national sire list, they didn't breed on to produce stallions at least as effective as themselves. There was one exception, but he is a story for the next chapter.

"When you talk about Bold Ruler," Capps said, "you go back to why Claiborne was so successful over so many generations. No stallion took over the operation so fully that he defined the farm. So when they

**SIR IVOR**

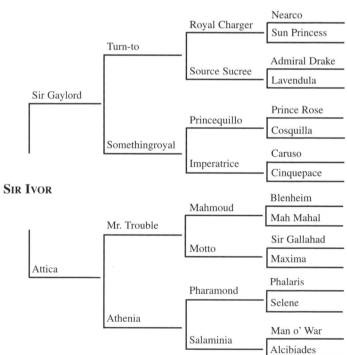

| | | | Nearco |
|---|---|---|---|
| | | Royal Charger | Sun Princess |
| | Turn-to | | Admiral Drake |
| Sir Gaylord | | Source Sucree | Lavendula |
| | | | Prince Rose |
| | | Princequillo | Cosquilla |
| | Somethingroyal | | Caruso |
| | | Imperatrice | Cinquepace |
| | | | Blenheim |
| | | Mahmoud | Mah Mahal |
| | Mr. Trouble | | Sir Gallahad |
| Attica | | Motto | Maxima |
| | | | Phalaris |
| | | Pharamond | Selene |
| | Athenia | | Man o' War |
| | | Salaminia | Alcibiades |

lost one like him, it was a big loss, but they took up the business the next day and went on as best they could. Then in time, the next great stallion would show up."

# The Next Generation

As with the loss of Nasrullah and of Princequillo, Claiborne weathered the loss of Bold Ruler, too.

Hancock had already been planning, not for the death of the world's greatest sire, but to find supplementary talent and to build up the stallion ranks at Claiborne to the greatest extent possible. To this end, he had Buckpasser and Damascus waiting in the wings, Le Fabuleux and Herbager as proven classic influences, and the outcross bloodlines from Australia and South America to mix with quick and sturdy American broodmares.

Before Bold Ruler died, Hancock was already searching out the best prospects available, and he landed a trio of champions who showed speed, early development, and high classic ability.

Sir Ivor was from the Claiborne stallion Sir Gaylord, and this horse – after his selection by Vincent O'Brien for Raymond Guest and subsequent successes in England and Ireland, and America – helped to change European perceptions of American bloodstock and racing prospects. Highweighted as a juvenile when he won the National Stakes in Ireland and the Grand Criterium in France, Sir Ivor was regarded as a talented two-year-old but not universally considered classic enough for Europeans. At three, after winning the 2,000 Guineas and Derby, Sir Ivor ended his career with a victory in Maryland's Washington D.C. International and was the toast of breeders here and abroad.

After spending his first two seasons at stud in Ireland, Sir Ivor returned to Kentucky and spent the rest of his career at Claiborne.

Among Sir Ivor's best racers were Ivanjica, winner of the Arc de Triomphe, Bates Motel (Santa Anita Handicap), Equanimity (Fantasy Stakes), Fascinating Girl (Santa Margarita), Godetia (Irish 1,000 Guineas and Oaks), Lady Capulet (Irish 1,000 Guineas), Miss Toshiba (Vanity

Courtesy Dell Hancock Photography

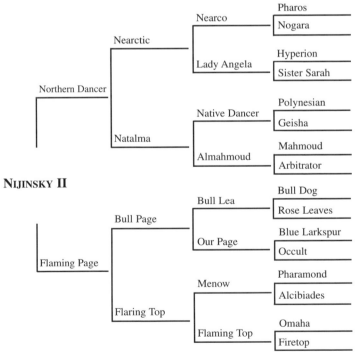

**NIJINSKY II**

Northern Dancer

- Nearctic
  - Nearco
    - Pharos
    - Nogara
  - Lady Angela
    - Hyperion
    - Sister Sarah
- Natalma
  - Native Dancer
    - Polynesian
    - Geisha
  - Almahmoud
    - Mahmoud
    - Arbitrator

Flaming Page

- Bull Page
  - Bull Lea
    - Bull Dog
    - Rose Leaves
  - Our Page
    - Blue Larkspur
    - Occult
- Flaring Top
  - Menow
    - Pharamond
    - Alcibiades
  - Flaming Top
    - Omaha
    - Firetop

Handicap), Optimistic Gal (Frizette, Matron, Spinster, Kentucky Oaks, Alabama), and Sweet Alliance (Kentucky Oaks).

Prior to Sir Ivor's successes, the Europeans assumed – contrary to any logical reasoning – that they bred the best classic racing stock in the world, even though they had sold off many of their best stallions and broodmares for the better part of three decades. Compiling pedigrees with layers of quality in the form of Blenheim, Teddy, and Nasrullah and then testing them for speed and toughness had produced in the American Thoroughbred a better and more versatile type of classic racer that took the European racing scene by storm.

Traditionalists admitted that the best Kentucky-bred racers had speed, but they doubted that Sir Ivor, Mill Reef, or Nijinsky had the depth and quality to win their classics. After those horses had slammed the best in Europe, breeders and owners from overseas queued up to buy everything American for racing abroad.

It's doubtful that Bull Hancock would take any credit for helping to create the international demand for American-bred racing stock. He was just trying to breed the best horses that he could imagine. And to do that, he had to have the best racing stock, and he found another example of this in the English Triple Crown winner Nijinsky.

The first great racehorse sired by Northern Dancer, Nijinsky was quite unlike his sire. Northern Dancer was so small as a yearling that his breeder, E.P. Taylor, was unable to sell him, despite his great balance and quality. In contrast, Nijinsky had inherited the size and substance of his dam, Flaming Page. As a result, Nijinsky attracted the notice of Vincent O'Brien, now buying yearlings regularly at the American auctions, and O'Brien selected Nijinsky for Charles Engelhard.

A horse of impressive stature and muscularity, Nijinsky swept through his juvenile season unbeaten. There were naturally doubters overseas that such a fast colt would relish the classic challenges of Newmarket and Epsom. After taking the first English Triple Crown since Bahram, Nijinsky was hailed a marvel.

Efforts by English breeders to secure him as a stallion failed, and the champion retired to stud at Claiborne. Before his success in the

St. Leger, Nijinsky had been acquired for stud by an American group led by Hancock with a record syndication of $5.44 million. The 32 shares were priced at $170,000 each, with Engelhard retaining 10 shares. The syndication value surpassed the prices paid previously for contemporary stallions Vaguely Noble ($5 million), Buckpasser, Dr. Fager ($3.2 million), Damascus ($2.56 million), and Sir Ivor ($2.08 million).

Expensive as it seemed, the price for Nijinsky was an utter bargain. The great racehorse proved a great sire, with his best offspring typically being exported to race abroad, where they won classics in England, Ireland, and France. Enough of the Nijinskys remained in the U.S. to race well here, and Kentucky Derby winner Ferdinand is his best-known domestic racer.

The year that Nijinsky won the English Triple Crown was 1970, and the best American juvenile that year was Hoist the Flag, a son of Preakness winner Tom Rolfe, who stood at Claiborne. A small and rather lightly made son of the international champion Ribot, Tom Rolfe had a tremendous first crop of racers, and Hoist the Flag was his best.

Although Hoist the Flag made only four starts at two, he finished first in each, was disqualified and placed last in the Champagne for interference early in the race when he was notably the best. The voters gave the award for ability, and Hoist the Flag went into his second season as a hot favorite to become an American Triple Crown winner.

Hoist the Flag won his 1971 debut at Bowie racecourse, then followed with a seemingly effortless seven-length victory in the Bay Shore at Aqueduct, in 1:21 for the seven furlongs. Tom Rolfe's son Droll Role was second, Jim French third, and Limit to Reason, who had inherited victory in the previous year's Champagne, was fourth.

On March 31, Hoist the Flag worked five furlongs and broke down in his right hind pastern and cannon. Veterinarians and an orthopedic surgeon were brought in, worked on the injured champion, and saved him.

Hoist the Flag proved an excellent stallion, with his best offspring being Alleged, twice the winner of the Arc de Triomphe, only once beaten in his racing career, and an important international sire.

From the first, Hoist the Flag showed that he could get champions, such as the leading juvenile filly Sensational. Whether on dirt or turf, short or long, the racing stock by Hoist the Flag showed speed and frequently the ability to carry it a classic distance.

Before his death in 1980, Hoist the Flag had become another in the amazing battery of world-class stallions standing at Claiborne Farm.

In 1970, he was simply another fine animal added to the array of stars at Claiborne. The accumulation of rich pedigrees, backed up with solid physiques and quality performances, made the breeding stock at Claiborne unrivalled. The stallions selected for Claiborne were good individuals, and as racing stock they had proven themselves exceptional in some way. Although Hancock was partial to the exceptionally talented classic stallion prospects, and with good reason, he consistently took chances by selecting an occasional horse who had outstanding qualities, like Double Jay, Nantallah, or Drone, but who fell short of the demands placed on the classic horse for some reason that Hancock could live with.

As a result, he kept working with the clay that forms the Thoroughbred, adding and developing and molding the forms and types, so that one day he would find the best horse possible. That was the goal of breeding racehorses at Claiborne.

When Bull Hancock set out to make Claiborne the best breeding farm in the world and a successful owner-breeder racing its own stock, did he ever wonder how high he would get? If he did, he never let on. He just kept on.

The statistics show that he bred 84 stakes winners and was four times the country's leading breeder (in 1958-59 and in 1968-69). Claiborne swelled from 2,100 acres to about 6,000 acres with 350 broodmares.

As part of his work and service to the sport and business, Hancock was a member of the Jockey Club, a voting trustee of the Keeneland Association, served on the Kentucky State Racing Commission, and was president of the American Thoroughbred Breeders Association.

With his many accomplishments, Bull Hancock's greatest desire was to breed and race his own Kentucky Derby winner. He ran two in the classic. Dunce was seventh in 1959, and in 1969, Dike was a good third to Majestic Prince and Arts and Letters against one of the best Derby fields in that decade.

Bull Hancock never won the Kentucky Derby, but both his sons did.

# CHAPTER THREE

# Changing of the Guard

The decade of the 1970s was much like the 1960s in terms of Claiborne's influence on racing and breeding. If anything, the farm's influence became more pronounced worldwide. Not only did Bold Ruler finally sire a classic winner, but that horse was Secretariat, the first American Triple Crown winner in a quarter of a century. A horse of exceptional beauty and athletic talent, Secretariat became a star to millions of horse-crazy teens and adults thanks to his presence on televisions and in magazines. In that regard, Secretariat was as important to the sport as he was for the commanding ability that allowed him to dominate racing for the two years he was on the track.

Furthermore, the sons of Bold Ruler began siring classic winners. Bold Commander's son Dust Commander won the 1970 Kentucky Derby. Cannonade (by Bold Bidder) won in 1974, the year after Secretariat. Then Foolish Pleasure (What a Pleasure), Bold Forbes (Irish Castle), and Seattle Slew (Bold Reasoning, by Bold Ruler's son Boldnesian) won the Derby in 1975, 1976, and 1977. Bold Forbes won both the Derby and the Belmont, and Seattle Slew went one better the following year to secure the second Triple Crown of the decade for a member of the Bold Ruler line. Spectacular Bid (Bold Bidder) won both the Kentucky Derby and Preakness and was Horse of the Year the next season at four before retiring to stud at Claiborne.

Amazing as it seems, the sires of all those classic winners were raised at Claiborne, except for Bold Reasoning. But he and his sire Boldnesian both stood at Claiborne. Yet during a decade that raised public awareness of Claiborne Farm to unprecedented levels, the farm had to survive changes that sent shocks through its foundations.

Not only did the world's preeminent sire, Bold Ruler, die on July 12, 1971, but the master of Claiborne, Bull Hancock, also fell victim to illness.

The death of Bull Hancock on September 14, 1972, was a shock to the horse business, to Claiborne, to his many friends and acquaintances, and most especially to his family.

Only 62 at the time of his death, Hancock was at the peak of his influence in the industry and had brought two decades of steady work with Claiborne to full ripeness.

The loss of a man of his stature was never going to be a simple thing for the horse business, but for the Hancock family it was very traumatic.

In addition to the natural pain of a grieving family, Seth Hancock said that the root of the problem was that his father's death "was all so sudden. I put him on a plane, I think it was the last day of July, to go to Saratoga. He was up there a couple of weeks, then they went to Scotland hunting, and he got to feeling poorly when he was in Scotland. They thought he had some sort of stomach infection. Flew him back to Vanderbilt and did surgery on him. Cancer. And he died about three weeks or a month after that."

The shortness of this time meant that there was no time for the family to come to an understanding of what was happening to them or to work with their father to smooth the transition of power and work.

The transition, considering the trouble everyone was going through, had some predictably rocky spots. Seth Hancock said, "Well, the bad part about it was that it was so sudden. He never really had a chance to say 'You do this, and you do that' " in terms of running the farm and making decisions about who took care of which tasks.

With regard to planning the running of the farm into the future, especially with regard to organization and a business plan, Seth Hancock said, "He had it set up, but he never really explained it to us. And it probably would have helped things if he could have explained what he did and why he did it. But he didn't, in that timetable."

There was a moment during the time when Bull Hancock was ill that he apparently came close to opening up the box of his plans for the future of Claiborne without himself and explaining the process to his family. Seth recalled that the family was in Nashville, and "we all went to see him one day. I'm going to say it was the 20th of August, and he wasn't out of it. He was all right. We went in there, and he sat up in bed, and he said, 'Well, you're all here. It's time we need to have a little family meeting.'

"And my mom smiled and said, 'Now, Bull, you're not feeling well. Now's not the time for that.' And I wished we'd had that family meeting. I don't know what he was going to say. I have no idea what he was going to say. But knowing him, I would expect he probably would have said, 'Now, this is the way it's set up, and this is what I want you all to do. So get out there and do it.'

"But we didn't have it, and he didn't say it. So I don't know what . . . So it was set up the way it was set up, and down the road we went."

Courtesy Dell Hancock Photography

Young Seth Hancock and his mother

As indicated through Hancock's will, Claiborne was converted to a family corporation, with each of the four children, Arthur, Clay, Seth, and Dell, being shareholders along with their mother Waddell. The will also suggested that the farm initially be run under the supervision of a trio of directors and a group of financial supervisors.

The elder Hancock had only come to manage Claiborne after a lengthy time of apprenticeship with his father and no doubt felt he knew the many pitfalls that had to be avoided for the farm to prosper consistently through the coming years. With directors and advisers to guide the family, Hancock also recommended in his will that Claiborne should return to selling its yearlings at auction.

With these arrangements directed by Hancock through his will, Claiborne wasn't likely to have many surprises. There also wasn't a great deal of room for differences of opinion, or even differing ideas of planning and execution. Seth recalled that "we started it, and Arthur wasn't satisfied with the way it was set up. And as I say, if it could have been explained to each of us why it was done the way it was done, it probably would have been easier on both of us. But he didn't like it. So he decided to go out on his own, and it's worked out great for everybody.

"He's had a hell of a run on his own, raised more good horses than anybody for what numbers he's had. Done a super job. And we've been able to keep this thing going."

Seth was named president of Claiborne by the farm advisers, and Arthur went his own way, founding the Stone Farm operation which has prospered so notably through the past four decades, breeding two Kentucky Derby winners (Gato del Sol and Fusaichi Pegasus) and racing a third (Sunday Silence).

At age 23, Seth was young for the responsibility and rigorous focus required to operate Claiborne and to make everything turn out well. But he did have the benefit of at least beginning a program of training that his father had arranged after Seth graduated from college.

Under this program of on-site experience, he was spending his initial winter working with the broodmares, then with the yearling operation breaking yearlings, then going to work with the farm manager for a year before a planned final year working directly with Bull.

At the time of his father's death, Seth said, "I was going to do a year with the farm manager, and the plan was, after I had done all that and was still on the right track, then he'd kinda take me under his wing. But we never got that far."

That time of working closely man to man with his father would have been a fascinating opportunity. It could have been the core of this book. But the uncertainties of life cut off Bull Hancock's decades of experience, intuitive understanding, and observation of racing and breeding before he passed it on to anyone else. We see it now through the perspective of time. Only our own observations of what Hancock did, which horses he chose and which he passed over, and how he managed them can indicate to us what he thought.

Nor had their father passed on his understanding to Arthur. After he'd graduated from Vanderbilt, Arthur had gone to work at the racetrack. "And then when he came back," Seth said, "I think Daddy thought 'Well, what the heck, let him learn on his own' and he set him up at Stone, where Arthur had several mares of his own, and a few clients, and he was learning through making his own mistakes, if he was making any, which he probably wasn't. That was to be his learning curve."

The learning curve in Thoroughbreds is long, occasionally steep, and you can get side-swiped along the way even if you are careful. Bull Hancock knew this as well as anyone. He had paid for his own mistakes, and perhaps he had a sense that mistakes, or experience from things that don't go perfectly, could be a masterful teacher. Whatever the case, from the way Hancock began his sons' education, he clearly expected to be there, both to oversee what went on and to cheer on their successes.

His early death changed all that, and essentially both Arthur and Seth were put under saddle and started out of the gate before they were green broke.

Both sons, however, also had the model of their father's actions and interests as they went about filling out their own careers in raising Thoroughbreds. As part of growing up around a father so consumed with Claiborne and horses, Seth said that "you'd hear him say things from time to time. You couldn't help it. Ever since I was a kid, I'd ride through the mares with him, and he might say, 'I like that mare,' and if you had enough sense, you'd look at that mare and say, 'What's he see in her?'

"You might ask him a question, 'Why do you like her?' And Arthur had the same experience I did. So it wasn't like we were totally on our own. But it wasn't like he ever came home and said, 'Well, let me tell you what I did today so that 20 years from now, you might apply some of this.' "

Seth and Arthur Hancock at the Keeneland sale.

Their education around horses began early in life. Seth said that most of the "time I ever rode around with him was when I was opening gates when I was 12, 13, 14. Then by the time I was 15 or 16, instead of opening gates, I might have been painting a gate or cutting the weeds out from under the gate."

Most of the Hancock sons' activity on the farm was practical work, not theoretical, and there was no sense of urgency in finding out the keys to their father's success as a businessman and horse breeder. This was compounded by the practical demands of being a teenager on a farm, where your labor was always of use somewhere. Bull Hancock rode the boys around with him when they were younger. "When I got old enough to have sense to ask about important things concerning horses or management, however, I was off doing something else," Seth said.

Seth and Arthur learned a great deal by observing their father, noting which stallions he stood at stud and which types of mares he had selected for the farm's broodmare band.

And when Seth took over Claiborne, he had a group of stallions that represented some of the finest racehorses and breeding stock in the world. Concerning his father's goals with the stallions at Claiborne, Seth said, "I heard him say many times that he was trying to acquire as many good young stud prospects as he could 'to build this farm up for you boys.' He had it built up. It was a roster you couldn't believe. Unbelievable. You had Forli, Damascus, Buckpasser, Herbager, Hoist the Flag. At that time, we thought Pronto was going to turn out to be something pretty good, but he turned out to be horrible. It was an amazing bunch of horses. Tom Rolfe was hot as a pistol when I took over. Hoist the Flag was in Tom Rolfe's first crop, and he had four good two-year-olds in that first crop."

Those juveniles included Droll Role (third in the Pimlico Futurity at two and the winner of the Washington D.C. International at four) and Run the Gantlet (winner of the Garden State Stakes at two, then the Washington D.C. International and Man o' War at three), as well as the crop's champion in Hoist the Flag.

A marvelous racehorse who finished first in each of his six starts, Hoist the Flag was disqualified from victory in the 1970 Champagne Stakes, just as Secretariat would be two years later. After an injury early in his three-year-old season sent Hoist the Flag to stud, he became an excellent sire in the U.S. and abroad.

Among the other promising young sires at Claiborne was the Bold Ruler horse Reviewer, who "had just served his first season after Daddy died," Seth said. "I know he did because he had some slight fertility problems in his first crop. He didn't quite put it all together that quick. He never was the most fertile horse in the world." Despite minor early problems with fertility, Reviewer became a good stallion, getting champion Ruffian in his first crop, and the stallion's other champion, Revidere, was bred by Claiborne in partnership with the Gamely Corp. of William Haggin Perry, who raced the filly.

**RIVA RIDGE**

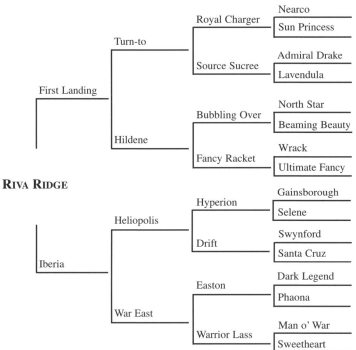

|  |  |  | Nearco |
|  | Royal Charger | |  |
|  |  | | Sun Princess |
| Turn-to | | | |
|  |  | | Admiral Drake |
|  | Source Sucree | |  |
|  |  | | Lavendula |
| First Landing | | | |
|  |  | | North Star |
|  | Bubbling Over | |  |
|  |  | | Beaming Beauty |
| Hildene | | | |
|  |  | | Wrack |
|  | Fancy Racket | |  |
|  |  | | Ultimate Fancy |
|  |  | | Gainsborough |
|  | Hyperion | |  |
|  |  | | Selene |
| Heliopolis | | | |
|  |  | | Swynford |
|  | Drift | |  |
|  |  | | Santa Cruz |
| Iberia | | | |
|  |  | | Dark Legend |
|  | Easton | |  |
|  |  | | Phaona |
| War East | | | |
|  |  | | Man o' War |
|  | Warrior Lass | |  |
|  |  | | Sweetheart |

92

In building the farm up and acquiring layers of the best bloodstock available, Bull Hancock had accomplished almost everything he had set out to do, and when Claiborne passed to the next generation, the farm's lineup of stallions was stacked, with bases loaded.

The first new stallion for the farm after Bull Hancock's death was Bold Reasoning. Seth noted that "Arthur and I actually syndicated Bold Reasoning together. We had a bunch of mares here on the farm for Mr. (Nelson Bunker) Hunt, and Daddy had told Mr. Hunt, 'Bunker, you've got all these foreign-bred things, got all this stamina. You've got to get some speed into it.'

"So Mr. Hunt had gone out, and on his own he'd purchased Bold Reasoning. He told us, 'Your dad said I needed some speed, and this was the fastest horse I could find. Do you all want to syndicate him?' Well, if you're going to breed your mares to him, sure. We did that together.

"He was the only freshman stallion we would have had for the '73 season, then Secretariat and Riva Ridge were the freshmen stallions for '74. Combined with what we already had, and those three, we were really rolling."

Those were exciting days for Claiborne, its staff, and clientele. One of the long-time clients at Claiborne was Christopher Chenery, who raced horses in the name of Meadow Stable. Chenery bred horses in Kentucky at Claiborne, as well as in Virginia at his farm, The Meadow. Chenery had bred the first champion by Princequillo, Preakness winner and Horse of the Year Hill Prince, and he also bred the first champion by Turn-to, the excellent two-year-old First Landing.

First Landing's best son was Riva Ridge, champion two-year-old colt in 1971 and winner of the Kentucky Derby and Belmont in 1972, and Meadow Stable's Secretariat came along the next year to win the Triple Crown. But by that time, however, Christopher Chenery had died.

Due to the accrual of estate taxes following the death of Christopher Chenery, the two classic winners from Meadow Stable were syndicated and went to stud at Claiborne. Secretariat was syndicated early in his three-year-old season of 1973 for a record price of $6.08 million, and the syndication of Riva Ridge followed that summer for a price not far below that of his regal stablemate.

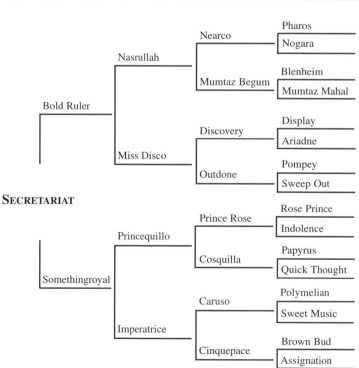

**SECRETARIAT**

| | | | |
|---|---|---|---|
| | | | Pharos |
| | | Nearco | Nogara |
| | Nasrullah | | Blenheim |
| | | Mumtaz Begum | Mumtaz Mahal |
| Bold Ruler | | | Display |
| | | Discovery | Ariadne |
| | Miss Disco | | Pompey |
| | | Outdone | Sweep Out |
| | | | Rose Prince |
| | | Prince Rose | Indolence |
| | Princequillo | | Papyrus |
| | | Cosquilla | Quick Thought |
| Somethingroyal | | | Polymelian |
| | | Caruso | Sweet Music |
| | Imperatrice | | Brown Bud |
| | | Cinquepace | Assignation |

At the time of his syndication, however, Riva Ridge was a champion and multiple classic winner. When Seth arranged the syndicate for Secretariat, the handsome son of Bold Ruler had been named Horse of the Year after a fine season at two but had not started at three.

The big colt won his first two starts, but the air seemed to get a lot thinner when Secretariat ran third in the Wood Memorial. With the colt syndicated for a record price due in part to his likely success in the classics, the two-week span between the Wood and the Kentucky Derby was a time of white-knuckled tension for those connected to the deal.

Puffed up with the usual backstretch rumors, some commentators, such as Las Vegas oddsmaker Jimmy the Greek Snyder, were quoting odds that Secretariat would not win the Derby, that he might not even race again.

On the day of the 99th Kentucky Derby, the chestnut son of Bold Ruler gave lengths to his opposition the first time past the wire, settling into last for a bit, then began picking up opponents one by one, two by two, until only Sham remained in front as the three-year-old colts drove into the homestretch. With his immense hindquarters bulging with strength, Secretariat powered past Sham to win the Derby and break the Churchill Downs track record set by Northern Dancer.

By the time he won the Triple Crown five weeks later, Secretariat had become an equine god, and prices for shares in the horse were being privately quoted for twice what had been paid only three months earlier.

Both of Meadow Stable's horses finished out their racing careers well. Secretariat was undeniable as Horse of the Year a second time, and Riva Ridge was named champion older horse.

Their acquisition to stand at Claiborne was an important statement that the farm was proceeding along the lines set out by Bull Hancock and that the future was both secure and prosperous.

The limelight of Secretariat's fame brought a price, of course. The farm had to institute a system of tours, guided by stallion grooms, to accommodate the horse's many fans. Previously, visitors to the farm could show themselves around and were expected to behave like reasonable people. But with such a large number of fans around the farm, especially with many unaccustomed to being around Thoroughbreds, extra care had to be taken for the protection of all.

In addition to the public response to Secretariat, another challenge came to the farm when the two horses were initially retired. In their initial fertility tests, both Secretariat and Riva Ridge produced semen that raised concerns when viewed under the microscope. Whether this was the effect of just a bit of immaturity or of life lived a little too much under a microscope is unclear.

Seth recollected "that when we had those initial problems with Secretariat and Riva Ridge, people told me 'Aw, hell, don't worry about that. They said Reviewer wasn't going to do any good, and he did fine.' But fertility-wise, those two horses, when they got over whatever was the initial problem, it (their fertility) wasn't a problem, but . . . they were very, very fertile horses. Both of them. They had good careers at stud. Secretariat wasn't Bold Ruler II, but nobody was."

Indeed, despite all the really good sons that Bold Ruler had sent to stud at respectable farms around the country, none was able to perform at their sire's lofty level. However, only a handful of horses have produced such a volume of stakes winners in the history of the breed. So, after Secretariat came to stud, "There was no way he could have lived up to expectations," Hancock said. "If every horse he'd sired had been a stakes winner, they'd have said they should have been champions. There was no way he could have lived up to what everybody thought he was going to be."

Even so, Secretariat really proved to be a solid sire, getting a Horse of the Year in Lady's Secret, a multiple classic winner in Risen Star (bred by Arthur Hancock), and the dams of the world-class sires Storm Cat, A.P. Indy, and Gone West. But all those accomplishments lay in the future as Secretariat and Riva Ridge began their lives as stallions in the winter of 1974. Also at Claiborne that winter, the first foals by the farm's sole freshman sire of 1973, Bold Reasoning, began to arrive.

Although not born at Claiborne, Seattle Slew was among Bold Reasoning's first crop of foals, and French highweight Super Concorde was in his second. The stallion died on April 24, 1975, after complications from colic. The son of Boldnesian and the Hail to Reason mare Reason to Earn had covered 28 mares in his third book prior to his death.

"And he might have been the best stallion that I, or that either one of us, had our hands on. But he died very prematurely," Seth said. "After two and a half crops. When he died, we thought, 'Well it's a damned shame because he was getting some right nice-looking horses. But at the time, Seattle Slew was then a yearling that sold for $17,000, and nobody knew he was Seattle Slew yet.

"But looking back on it, the horse was way more than a one-shot wonder, and I think he was probably going to be one heck of a stallion. Super Concorde (highweight juvenile colt in France where he was a Group 1 winner) was a really good horse, and that was from a limited book. It was a not a great big book, probably big by those standards, maybe 50 mares, but those were $5,000 stud fees that were paid. But he was going to be big time."

With hindsight, the loss of Bold Reasoning was a serious blow for racing and for Claiborne, but those are among the tough breaks of the horse business. With the loss of Bold Reasoning as with many other things, it is easy to wonder what might have happened. But Hancock provided some leavening to that line of speculation, saying that "if Seattle Slew hadn't come along, he wouldn't have been Bold Reasoning. There are two sides to every coin."

In the spring of 1974, the coin was mostly coming up heads for Claiborne. Secretariat and Riva Ridge were getting their mares in foal, the proven stallions were prospering, and Claiborne had a colt named Judger that was the favorite for the Kentucky Derby.

Seth had purchased the colt out of the dispersal of the Claiborne racing stable. Dell Hancock recalled that when the young stock was coming up at auction, "Seth liked Judger. He was by Damascus, wasn't bringing very much money, and buying him was a real boost for Seth and his confidence. We were just kids."

In addition to being by Claiborne stallion Damascus, whose early racers were doing quite well, Judger was out of the good Court Martial mare Face the Facts. During the spring of his three-year-old season,

Judger won both the Florida Derby and the Blue Grass, then started favorite as part of an entry from trainer Woody Stephens for the Kentucky Derby. Judger ran eighth behind entrymate Cannonade.

## Selecting Stallions and Mares

Despite that loss, Judger had done enough to earn a place at stud, and he retired to stand at Claiborne. Then as now, Seth Hancock has certain criteria he prefers when selecting stallions for the farm.

He said, "I still look for the same things I've always looked for, and I haven't changed. The things I've always thought were important I still feel are important, and we'll keep trying to get those same kind of stallions in here.

"The first thing, I think, is they better come from a good family. Strong Hope didn't run at two, but I think he'll be a hell of a stallion. He was fast. But if you say, 'I'm not taking a horse that didn't show two-year-old form, then you don't take Strong Hope, but you're out of your mind, in my view. Some people would mention speed or early development first, but I would mention pedigree first.

"Of course, now, you can have all the pedigree in the world, but if you don't have some performance to back it up, you're not going to be able to attract any mares. And when you look down that leading sire list, most all really, really good stallions have a pretty good pedigree.

"Some can say, 'Seattle Slew had no pedigree,' and at the time he was running, he didn't. But then it filled in behind him. There's a lot of good horses that came from that family."

Seattle Slew, out of stakes winner My Charmer, looked like an exceptional horse from an average sort of family at the time he was burning up the tracks and winning 14 of his 17 starts. But the family had some depth. "It was a young family," Hancock said. "He was out of a stakes winner. His dam was a producing machine."

In addition to producing Seattle Slew as her first foal, My Charmer later foaled Lomond (by Northern Dancer), who won the 2,000

Guineas at Newmarket in 1983 and also ran second in the Irish 2,000 Guineas, and in 1985 her Nijinsky yearling brought a record price of $13.1 million at the Keeneland July sale. Later named Seattle Dancer, this horse won the Group 2 Gallinule Stakes in Ireland and was second in the Group 1 Grand Prix de Paris. In all, six of My Charmer's first eight foals earned black type on the racetracks of the world, and she marked herself and her branch of the Myrtlewood family with great distinction.

Selecting mares and developing families is a subtle art, and both Bull Hancock and his father are credited with having a definite inclination toward a type of mare with good size, with length and depth through the body, a wide but yet feminine broodmare. Seth Hancock adds a definite dislike to the art of selecting broodmares. He said, "I don't want those big, masculine ones. I don't really like them, but there's many a type between the small, typey ones and the great big, masculine ones."

Even though he doesn't generally like the big, rough mare, Claiborne has had some that lay outside this guideline. Hancock said that "now in the early days, Face the Facts was a huge mare that Gamely and Daddy had, and Gamely herself was a huge mare, a great big thing, but for whatever reason, Face the Facts had Judger and was a pretty good broodmare, but the family didn't breed on. And Gamely didn't really have too much of anything, and her branch of the family kinda died out. Don't know why, but it did. But at times, there were bigger mares here."

During the 1970s, Gamely also had Revidere, a champion racer by Reviewer, also the sire of Ruffian. Hancock was quick to note the differences in the two champion fillies: "Ruffian was big, but she was elegant. Revidere was big, but she was pretty rough." Revidere's size and lack of obvious athleticism made it difficult for even her trainer to determine how good she was early in her career. Hancock recalled that "they were going to run Revidere in maiden claiming $35,000 before they ever started her. And they said, 'Aw hell, we better run her in straight maidens just to make sure we ain't making a mistake.' She hadn't shown that much in the morning."

Revidere made up in robustness what she lacked in finesse, but her qualities on the racetrack did not really translate into producing horses of equal ability after she became a broodmare. Hancock said that Revidere was a "big, masculine mare" and a "bad broodmare" because "she didn't get that many foals for one, and she never had what you'd say was a really good-looking foal."

Another sizable mare that Gamely and Claiborne bred was Number. Hancock was quick to distinguish here, though. "She was big enough, but she wasn't huge. She took more after her dam, Special, than she did Nijinsky."

Most of the Nijinskys were big and preferred to race longer distances on turf. Hancock said they were "just not the physicals to be quick and early." Some of the Nijinskys built along more medium-sized lines showed greater versatility, maturing more quickly and sometimes switching back and forth from turf to dirt.

Among the positive criteria for selecting mares, Hancock notes that "like the stallion, they better have some pedigree, no matter what they look like. But then again, a lot of times, when you see one that's an outstanding physical, you might think she doesn't have enough pedigree. But that might be the pedigree that's getting ready to blossom. Because her good looks and her presence had to come from somewhere. It might be the one that's just getting ready to pop."

Claiborne has certainly hit the bull's eye with families they have developed over the past half-century. Among the best-known of these are the Rough Shod family of champion Moccasin, which is also the family of the leading international sires Nureyev and Sadler's Wells. Many of these individuals have been sold out of the Claiborne broodmare band due to the emphasis on selling the yearling crops during the early years after Bull Hancock's death.

Additionally, Claiborne has sold off other families held in partnership. When Claiborne dispersed the Gamely Corp. mares in the years following the death of William Haggin Perry, those producers were an outstanding group of broodmares. They all had pedigree, most had some good performance, and as physicals, they were smooth, neat, well-balanced mares. Not surprisingly, they brought very large sums of money for the partners, with several of the mares going to the Coolmore operation of John Magnier.

As an international stallion entrepreneur, Magnier has profited from the sales of Claiborne families over the decades to an unprecedented extent. Among the best stock that has collected in the Coolmore bloodstock empire are Sadler's Wells, his dam Fairy Bridge, and the top-class English sprinter and sire Thatch.

Fairy Bridge was sold at the yearling sales in 1976 and did not make a large mark as a racehorse. Retained as a broodmare, she laid the foundations of Coolmore's world domination. Her first foal was Sadler's Wells, who ranks with Nearco, Hyperion, St. Simon, and Blandford as one of the greatest European sires of this century or any other. And her second foal was the once-raced Fairy King (also by Northern Dancer like Sadler's Wells), who became a significant stallion in Ireland, as well. In fact, Fairy King was the only one of the mare's first six offspring that did not earn black type.

Yet if Bull Hancock had not died, the dam of Sadler's Wells would never have gone to Ireland. With regard to "that Bold Reason filly out of Special (Fairy Bridge)," Hancock said, "if Daddy hadn't passed away, she'd never have been sold." She was the kind of mare who makes a farm.

Among the types of mares that Hancock generally weeds out of the Claiborne broodmare band are unraced mares. "We didn't keep too many unraced mares," he said, "unless we thought that they had talent, and for whatever reason, they didn't get to show it."

One example of a mare with ability but little performance was the dam of Fairy Bridge, the Forli mare Special. Hancock said, "I heard them say this one time about Special, 'Oh, she could really run. We ran her one time, and she bled real bad. But she had a lot of talent.' Well, I'm glad I heard that because when I took over and I looked down and saw that Special ran one time and didn't do any good, if Mr. Perry had said, 'We need to sell four or five mares,' I might have said, 'What about Special?' but I'd heard that about her, from somewhere. So I would never have shucked her just because of remembering that. And look what she turned out to be. Unbelievable."

Yes, indeed.

As nothing more than the dam of Fairy Bridge, Special would have lived up to her name. But this daughter of Thong, the stakes-placed full sister to Moccasin, did much more. Her third foal was Nureyev, a small but beautifully made son of Northern Dancer. Sold by Claiborne for $1 million as a yearling in 1978, Nureyev finished first in all three of his starts but was disqualified from victory in the 2,000 Guineas of 1980. Retired to stud, he became a sire of great international significance, especially with his racers in England and France.

In addition, Special produced Number and Bound, a pair of daughters by Nijinsky who became successful racehorses and producers for Claiborne. As part of the Gamely dispersal, they sold to Coolmore.

Of the notable horses Claiborne sold, Hancock reasoned that "if my father had lived another 10 years, and we hadn't sold Caerleon and we hadn't sold Nureyev, the difference would have been unbelievable. But that's the way it is."

A foal of 1980, Caerleon was yet another top-quality racehorse by Nijinsky bred by Claiborne. Hancock described him as "about as good a looking horse as you'd ever want to see. And he was not a typical Nijinsky, one of those big, rough-looking, gangly things. He was a typey, beautiful-looking horse."

But the change in Claiborne's policy from raising and racing its own horses to selling "was mandated in his will. Stability. You know if you're selling, you're going to have cash coming in. If you're racing, it can be very cyclical. You might go three, four, five years and not do any good, and boom, then here come two good horses to carry the load.

"His fear, I guess, was that if we had those two, three, or four dry years right after he passed away, we might get into bad enough shape where this place wouldn't make it. The bottom line is that here we are 32 years later, and we're still in business. And I'm sure that having worked so hard to build it up, he was surely very hopeful that it would carry on for a while."

One of the horses who helped to carry the farm after the elder Hancock's death was Horse of the Year Round Table. A son of Princequillo and a champion in a time of great champions, Round Table proved an outstanding sire, getting European classic winner Baldric, European champion Apalachee, the top American mare Drumtop, as well as a host of other stakes winners.

Round Table was the leading sire in North America in 1972, and he became a perennial leader among broodmare sires, with Caerleon being one of the best performers out of a Round Table mare.

Although an outstanding sire, Round Table did not have the extraordinary dominance of Bold Ruler. But year after year, the Round Tables were winning races, taking home good stakes, and then going on to become good producers.

Round Table and some of the rising stars at Claiborne were important figures in this transitional period at Claiborne. By the early 1980s, Hancock had had enough of the yearling sales. He wanted Claiborne to be back in the game as an owner and breeder.

## The Change is Complete

Part of the challenge that Hancock had to work through in his early years at Claiborne was carrying on his father's plans, making sure the ship went smoothly, and then also plotting the course for the future on his own. To forge the path to the future with Claiborne, Hancock had to acquire more premier stallions and, with luck, breed some top-class racehorses.

Two of the most important stallion acquisitions that allowed Claiborne to proceed with the same strength and success that it had already known came to the farm in unexpected ways.

Both Danzig and Mr. Prospector came to the farm through new associations that Hancock formed. He said, "My father never knew Peter Brant. My father never knew Henryk de Kwiatkowski, either. He did know Woody, obviously," who trained for Claiborne and also developed Danzig for de Kwiatkowski.

"Those two stallions would be the ones" that moved Claiborne forward into the 1980s, and "Peter Brant was big-time responsible for Mr. Prospector coming here," Hancock said. "He knew Mr. Savin. He called

**MR. PROSPECTOR**

| | | | Unbreakable |
| | | Polynesian | Black Polly |
| | Native Dancer | | Discovery |
| | | Geisha | Miyako |
| Raise a Native | | | Teddy |
| | | Case Ace | Sweetheart |
| | Raise You | | American Flag |
| | | Lady Glory | Beloved |
| | | | Nearco |
| | | Nasrullah | Mumtaz Begum |
| | Nashua | | Johnstown |
| | | Segula | Sekhmet |
| Gold Digger | | | Reigh Count |
| | | Count Fleet | Quickly |
| | Sequence | | Bull Dog |
| | | Miss Dogwood | Myrtlewood |

me and said, 'Seth, what do you think about Mr. Prospector?' I told him he's a hell of a stallion. He said, 'He's gonna leave Florida.' And I said, 'Aw, how are you going to get him out of Florida?'

"And he said, 'Mr. Savin's an older man, and he knows how good Mr. Prospector is, and he's getting worried to death with people trying to buy him. And he's going to leave. He's going to sell his shares, and if you'll arrange for those shares to be bought by people in Kentucky, and if you call a vote, they'll vote unanimously to move.'

"This was late in the year, and I said, 'You can't get anything done for the next season.'

And he said, 'No, but if you buy the shares now and get them placed and let him go through the season down there, when you call for the vote next June, he'll come here.'

"So I asked, 'How do you know all this?' and he said, 'I know this guy, and he's got two shares,' " and as a result, Brant had an inside track to what was happening with the Mr. Prospector syndicate.

"I think there were seven shares that Mr. Savin owned," Hancock recalled. "And I probably called Mr. Savin and asked him what he wanted for them, and he wanted $3.5 million for the seven shares. Claiborne took one, Claiborne and Mr. Perry took one, Mr. Phipps took one, I think Ed Cox took one, I think Peter took two or three. Anyway, they got snapped up pretty quick.

"And it was just like Peter said. They called for the vote next June. Well, hell, I guess we called for it, and it was 39 to 1 to move. So he came up here. I think he actually bred a mare or two up here that June. A couple of the guy's mares hadn't caught, and they sent them up here to try to catch them."

The transfer of Mr. Prospector to Kentucky was an enormous shift of influence. Within a few more years, other leading Florida stallions, such as Fappiano, also shifted their residence to Kentucky.

The initial Kentucky shareholders in Mr. Prospector profited by getting a major stakes winner, sometimes two or three. And the stallion's yearlings began to bring enormous prices at the yearling sales.

At about the same time as the transfer of Mr. Prospector, an unbeaten son of Northern Dancer joined the Claiborne stallion roster. This horse had been trained by Woody Stephens, had shown amazing speed on the track, but lacked one thing from a typical Claiborne stallion's resume: he had never won a stakes.

And Hancock was not wild about the idea of standing him.

Even now, after Danzig has been pensioned following an illustrious breeding career, Hancock laid his cards on the table regarding the stallion's purchase and breeding career. "He probably bred better than what he was himself. If someone said, 'He's a little on the dumpy side,' I wouldn't argue with them. He was kinda round-shouldered. I thought he outbred himself. And he produced horses that were sound, although he was not. I guess Woody might have said he was so fast he couldn't keep him sound."

In time, the dumpy little horse who couldn't stay sound became one of the great sires in the world. Knowing this, Hancock said, "Course, I'm stupid enough to buy him. I said that he wasn't very sound. And Woody said, 'Well, Seth, he was on them other three legs. He just had that one knee.' I guess that's probably his way of selling him to me, but I'll bite.

"But he said, you know, he would have been a sound horse. I'll never forget it, but he told me, 'My brother Bill had him in Aiken and had that damned boy Peaches getting on him, and Peaches must have weighed a hundred and fifty pounds, and he started having trouble with that knee then, and that's what got him.' "

Danzig's left knee, the one he had to lean on racing around a turn, prevented him from having a more successful racing career. But the story worked its magic. Hancock continued talking to the trainer about his pet racer who needed to become a stallion.

Hancock said, "Woody sold him to me. I wasn't going to take him. It was all Woody. I wasn't going to take him. I just said, 'Woody, I can't do any good with him.' He said, 'Well, you do what you want, but he was a fast son of a gun, and I believe he'll make a good sire. And Henryk's going to breed good mares to him. And I wish you'd take him.' "

Despite Woody's assurances, Hancock nearly passed on the horse. "I pretty much said no, and he called me, and he said 'I'm gonna run that filly of yours up here on Thursday,' and I said 'Good, I know you like her,' And he said, 'Yep, I think she'll win.' He said, 'I'm gonna put that filly of Henryk's in there, that Nijinsky filly that I bought out of Rosetta Stone. He's coming out here, and I think she'll win too. They're gonna split the race. Why don't you come up here.'

"So I said 'Well, all right, I'll come up there.' He said, 'You meet me and Henryk in the trustees' room, and we'll have lunch, then we'll watch these two fillies run.' So I said, 'All right.'

"So I met them in the trustees' room, and Henryk had to tell me all about this and that; that's the way he was. He'd talk and you'd listen. Then finally, Woody in so many words, said, 'Well, Henryk, that's enough of that. We've got to figure out what to do about Danzig because he's through, and it's time for him to go home.'

"Henryk said something, and then Woody said, 'Seth, how much can you give, what's the best you can do on this horse?'

"And I said, 'Well, maybe we can stand him for $20[,000] and we can sell shares for $80[,000]. And that would make him worth 36 times $80[,000], whatever that is.'

"And he said, 'Henryk, you better take it.'

"And Henryk rared up, 'You gotta deal,' and stuck his hand out. And that's one thing about him. That was the end of it. It wasn't gorgeous, but that's the way it was. If Woody hadn't called me up there, I don't know where the horse would have gone. But he wouldn't have come here.

"Both of those fillies won, too, and one of them was De La Rose." The Nijinsky filly out of the Round Table mare Rosetta Stone was named De La Rose and became a very high-class racer. A stakes winner at two and three, she won the Hollywood Derby over colts, was second in the Kentucky Oaks. As a broodmare, De La Rose produced Grade 1 winner Conquistarose (by Conquistador Cielo) for de Kwiatkowski.

So Danzig came to stand at Claiborne, and he got a good book of mares because "he had raced in New York, Woody was talking him up,

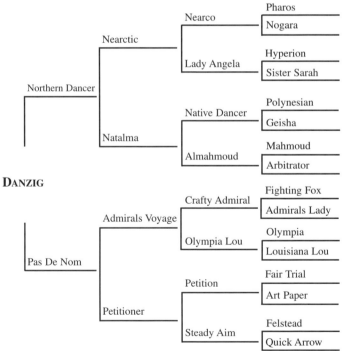

**DANZIG**

| | | | Pharos |
| | | Nearco | Nogara |
| | Nearctic | | Hyperion |
| Northern Dancer | | Lady Angela | Sister Sarah |
| | | | Polynesian |
| | | Native Dancer | Geisha |
| | Natalma | | Mahmoud |
| | | Almahmoud | Arbitrator |
| | | | Fighting Fox |
| | | Crafty Admiral | Admirals Lady |
| | Admirals Voyage | | Olympia |
| Pas De Nom | | Olympia Lou | Louisiana Lou |
| | | | Fair Trial |
| | | Petition | Art Paper |
| | Petitioner | | Felstead |
| | | Steady Aim | Quick Arrow |

he was a Northern Dancer, and the Northern Dancer sons were starting to do well," Hancock summarized.

Danzig rewarded their faith, and that of the breeders who used the stallion, by siring champion Chief's Crown in his first crop, along with Grade 1 winner and Kentucky Derby second Stephan's Odyssey, and a horde of other stakes winners and high-class racers.

Among the champions sired by the chunky bay son of Northern Dancer are Dayjur, Dance Smartly, Polish Precedent, Anaaba, Pas de Reponse, and Danehill. The latter has been Danzig's most successful son at stud, and other sons, such as Green Desert, Anaaba, Belong to Me, Pine Bluff, and Boundary have sired high-class runners in Europe or America.

Of those, Claiborne raced Boundary and stands him. But the best Danzig that Claiborne bred was Lure, twice the winner of the Breeders' Cup Mile and one of the best horses never voted a champion. Racing in Claiborne's colors, Lure was a Grade 1 winner at three, four, and five.

A game and zestful racer, Lure showed his best form racing on turf at distances from eight to 10 furlongs. Sound and handsome, he was an outstanding stallion prospect when retired to Claiborne at the end of 1994. Unfortunately, infertility prevented the horse from making a significant mark as a stallion.

Although Lure was able to get only a small number of his mates in foal and champion sprinter Dayjur proved a serious disappointment as a sire, Danzig has bred on well, especially in Europe and Australia, where the majority of racing is conducted on turf.

In 2004, Danzig was pensioned from stud duty after a fantastic career, and he is, according to bloodstock commentator Bill Oppenheim, the last of the great stallions. By that, he meant that Danzig was a stallion who never bred very large books of mares and yet had immense and lasting success. As a result, Danzig is purely a great stallion.

Hancock agreed: "He's the last of the stallions who had a small, managed book and got darn near 20 percent stakes winners. He was a good-looking, not pretty looking, fast horse who got great runners."

# The More Things Change

After nearly a decade's success at the sales with the Claiborne consignments, Hancock and the Claiborne advisers were ready to make a change. Rather than produce top-class stock and see them become champions and top breeding animals for other operations, Claiborne went back to a version of the program that Bull Hancock had developed by keeping some of its horses to race while selling off interests in each year's crop of yearlings.

After selling the entire Claiborne yearling crop for several years, Hancock decided to retain the fillies beginning in 1977, and then he decided to form a partnership that would purchase the yearling colts and race them, with Claiborne keeping an interest.

Hancock said, "We took the colts from the Claiborne-Gamely mares and syndicated them. Mr. Perry kept a quarter, Claiborne kept a quarter, Peter Brant took a quarter, Ed Cox took an eighth, and Dell and I each took a sixteenth individually."

This was a bold move financially, as these were some of the most valuable horses that the farm bred. But Hancock noted that is how "we started Raceland Stable, and there were nine colts we put in the partnership the first year. Swale was in the first bunch."

A near-black colt from the second crop by Triple Crown winner Seattle Slew, Swale came along "the first year we shifted out of the sales ring. That was big," Hancock said.

To divide the colts for racing, the partners in Raceland took turns selecting them as yearlings, and Hancock said Swale "was the fifth colt taken. There were four in that bunch that were better thought of than him."

People began to think a lot more of the sleek dark colt after he won the Futurity, Young America, and Breeders' Futurity at two.

Then at three, Swale delivered on the decades of promise, the years of work, hope, and expectation. He won the Kentucky Derby in 1984.

Both in his accomplishments and in his bloodlines, Swale was a colt of destiny for Claiborne. Bull Hancock had imported Swale's fourth dam, the Hyperion mare Highway Code, in 1950 after purchasing her from Lord Astor. The mare's first mate at Claiborne was Nasrullah, serving his first Kentucky book in 1951, and the resulting foal was Courtesy, who was second in the Ashland and a really useful filly. At stud Courtesy proved a lot more than useful.

She produced three stakes winners, all by Round Table, and two stakes-placed horses. Knightly Manner won nine stakes, Respected won the Santa Ynez, and Dignitas won the Strub. They were all very solid racehorses. Courtesy's second foal was the Double Jay mare Continue, who won five of seven starts but no black type.

Like her dam, Continue did even better as a producer than as a racer. The mare brought forth five stakes winners, and two of them were fillies, Tuerta (by Forli) and File (by Tom Rolfe). Both had major roles to play in creating the next generation of successful racehorses at Claiborne, as Tuerta became the dam of Swale and two other stakes horses, including Belmont Stakes third Illuminate, and File produced champion Forty Niner, who ran a game second in the Kentucky Derby and later led the general sire list.

Tuerta, whose name in Spanish means "blind in one eye," was the last stakes winner to carry the Claiborne silks prior to Bull Hancock's death. Tuerta's ability to overcome her impairment and her significance as their father's last stakes winner made Tuerta a favorite with the Hancock family.

When she produced the farm's first Kentucky Derby winner, Tuerta had carried the Hancocks to an unprecedented high.

Although he lost the Preakness, Swale bounced back to win the Belmont. A few days later, however, Swale died of an apparent heart attack.

"There's no telling how good he'd have been later on because he was just a big skinny colt when he won the Derby and Belmont," Hancock said. "We were going to give him some time off, and I think he would have come back in the fall a good, good horse, and I think he would have come back as a four-year-old a great horse because he would have filled out by then."

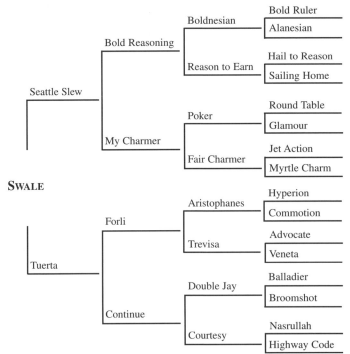

**SWALE**

- Seattle Slew
  - Bold Reasoning
    - Boldnesian
      - Bold Ruler
      - Alanesian
    - Reason to Earn
      - Hail to Reason
      - Sailing Home
  - My Charmer
    - Poker
      - Round Table
      - Glamour
    - Fair Charmer
      - Jet Action
      - Myrtle Charm
- Tuerta
  - Forli
    - Aristophanes
      - Hyperion
      - Commotion
    - Trevisa
      - Advocate
      - Veneta
  - Continue
    - Double Jay
      - Balladier
      - Broomshot
    - Courtesy
      - Nasrullah
      - Highway Code

Both Swale and Slew o' Gold were bred by Claiborne in a foal-sharing arrangement with Equusequity Stable, the partnership of the Hills and Taylors who had raced Seattle Slew and had retained a significant stake in the Triple Crown winner and champion. Champion Slew o' Gold, from Seattle Slew's first crop, was a similar type of horse to Swale and went from being a good three-year-old in the first half of the year to a really good one in the second half. Hancock said, "I think Swale would have done the same thing, except he probably would have been even better because he was better early."

After breeding two champions by Seattle Slew, Claiborne had relatively little access to the horse afterward, as he became one of the world's most expensive and sought-after stallions. The dam of Slew o' Gold was Alluvial, "one of the nicest Buckpasser mares," Hancock said. A Gamely Corp. mare, "Alluvial was 16.1 probably. She was a chestnut Buckpasser type" with elegance and scope.

In addition to the death of Swale in the mid-1980s, Claiborne also faced challenges to the health of one of its premier sires, Nijinsky. "He foundered, and then he had lymphangitis," Hancock recalled. "One year, when that founder was pretty acute, we bred him in his barn down there. We put down a surface, a Tartan surface, because they said, 'You can't give him exercise.' So we just led him out of his stall, bred him right there in the hallway of the barn, and put him right back in his stall."

Dire as the problems were, Nijinsky overcame them and continued to be a top-flight stallion.

Just as before, in the early to mid-1980s, Claiborne continued trying to select top stallions, only the prices had changed.

Whereas $5 million was enough to buy Nijinsky when he retired to stud, sums four to six times that amount were required to secure top-tier commercial stallion prospects in the '80s. In that white-hot stallion market, the farm syndicated champion Devil's Bag, as well as Horse of the Year Conquistador Cielo. They proved to be useful sires, but not premier stallions like Danzig and Mr. Prospector.

Again in the early 1990s, when the top young sire Unbridled seemed likely to sell overseas, Claiborne and a consortium of committed breeders stepped in, purchased the stallion, and sent him to stud at Claiborne. Despite his premature death in 2001, Unbridled has proven to be one of the most dependable sources of classic ability in American breeding.

Throughout this period of change and intense commercialization in the stallion market, Claiborne has run counter to the breeding businessman's inclination to create 200-mare books, to shuttle stallions, to drain every dollar possible out of the horse.

These facts of life in the commercial world have meant further changes for Claiborne, however. The stallion roster notably has shrunk since the heydey of production in the mid- to late 1980s. Hancock said, "At one time we had 27 stallions, but that was probably when there was 53,000 foals. When it settled back down around the 35,000 foal number, we cut it down to 18. Now, we've only got 11, and that's not enough."

The change in the marketplace and the way business is done has "prevented us from being able to compete on a lot of horses. We're not quite as much in the past as we used to be because not long ago, 80 or 90 mares was all we wanted for a stallion. I can tell you now, we'll go to probably a 120 or a 125. But I'm not going above that."

Taking these changes into account, Hancock said, "We hope to build this thing back up to where we've got 15-16 or 17-18 stallions." Despite wanting more stallions in a changing world and economy, he said, "We're not just going to take horses just for the sake of taking them. And we're not going to compromise our principles."

The financial considerations that figure into selecting and purchasing a stallion are subtle and complex. The psychology of breeders and the economic structure of purses and the sales tend to dictate what farms can afford to spend for stallions and then hope to recover if the horse has average success.

Hancock believes these considerations are a reflection of "the state of the game. You take a horse like Pleasantly Perfect, who's obviously a really good racehorse, a sound horse, a pretty damned good pedigree. Probably not going to get much of a chance as a stallion, and the reason being that not many people would breed to him. It [taking him at Claiborne] would have to be a giant leap of faith on the part of guy like me because I'd have to breed 15-20 mares to him. When you've only got 50 mares, you can't do something like that because if he doesn't make it, you're dead.

"And we know that only about one out of five do make it. So if you keep taking those horses out of the gene pool, down the road what are we going to have? Nothing but a bunch of horses by fast milers, probably most of them are going to have Mr. Prospector or Northern Dancer. The gene pool's going to shrink, shrink, shrink. I don't know where we're going to be 20 years from now.

"I'm not saying that [reluctance of breeders to use late-maturing stayers] is wrong. I took one called Go for Gin, and he was a Pleasantly Perfect type horse. We bred a few mares to him ourselves and tried to make him, and we finally ran up the flag. He's gone to Maryland. He didn't get it done."

Staying horses have occasionally been made into successful stallions, but in most cases over the past two decades, that has taken an owner or two with deep pockets and the willingness to commit good mares to the stallion over a period of years. Probably the most successful horse of that type is the Nureyev stallion Theatrical, whom Allen Paulson, almost single-handedly, proved as an outstanding sire of racers best-suited to middle distance racing on turf. But Theatrical is the exception who proves the rule.

Hancock admits that the "game's gotten so commercial it's tough. And even at the commercial end, you can take a good yearling up there, and if he doesn't look like he's going to be a good two-year-old, you can get him sold, but you won't get a whole lot of money for him."

If you want to make great sales consistently, a yearling "better look like one of them that can go a quarter of a mile in :21 so that the pinhookers will like him, or be one that you can run in the Hopeful at Saratoga so that the people that are getting in the business now will like him, but that's just the way of the world."

As a result of commercial and economic constraints, a farm like Claiborne that supports itself through breeding is locked into buying a horse who is commercial, who will have wide appeal, but is not so extravagantly priced that he blows out all those considerations.

One avenue for a farm to avoid some of the economic pitfalls is to breed its own stallions. That is what Claiborne has done the past 20 years, getting Swale, Forty Niner, Lure, and Pulpit among its topmost prospects. Tremendous ill luck took two of those out of the mix, but Forty Niner and Pulpit produced successes at Claiborne.

In addition to the economic benefits of having bred and raced the horse, the farm also owns the horse outright when he goes to stud. Then, "if he's ours, we can manage him in the way we see that'll give him every opportunity to make it. The fee [for Forty Niner and Pulpit] was set at such a level that they would attract an awful lot of applications, and we could pick and choose. I think you'd have to say Forty Niner made it, and I think you'd have to say that Pulpit has made it. So, doing it the way we did it, we're two for two."

But horses of that caliber come along infrequently, and a stallion operation has to acquire other horses. To do that requires a good deal of judgment, and one of the factors to assess is the nature of the horse's owner. Hancock said, "if a man who owns the horse isn't one that you really think will buy in to what you're trying to preach to him, then maybe it's a horse you should syndicate. If a man owns a horse, you have to do what he wants you to do, but if he comes to you and says, 'You tell me what to do with this horse,' and then you say I think we ought to stand him for $40,000, and he says that he's thinking more of 50 or 60, then you're better off going and setting up a syndicate. Get him some money in his pocket and let other people support the stallion, 'cause at 50 or 60, you perhaps don't think you can round up the right kind of people or the right kind of mares to get the job done the way it needs to be done."

A further complication of the commercial market is that "after the first two years that a horse has been at stud," Hancock said, "it's like 'Call me when he makes it,' because there's 20 others that have just been retired, and they ain't got no chinks in their armor. They're undefeated, untied, and unscored upon. But that's the commercial end. A guy doesn't want to breed the third year and take a chance on leading some yearling up there by some sire that everybody says, 'Aw, he ain't doing nothing.'"

For anyone who believes that operating a stallion operation is simple, Hancock summed it up: "It's a tough game."

Due to the demands of the marketplace and the economics of racing, Hancock said, "We're more commercial now than we were a few years ago," and in the first years of the 21st century, Claiborne has made a transition back to selling a large portion of its annual yearling crop.

"We had to decide whether to try to race 65 or 70 horses and disperse them among a bunch of different trainers," Hancock said. "I wasn't real comfortable with that, and truth be told, the purse structure at a lot of tracks was beginning to deteriorate. And it has continued to do so, whether people want to admit it or not.

"If it hasn't deteriorated, it has stayed stagnant. So right now, I'd be very uncomfortable trying to race a great big stable of horses. Now, we've got 32 horses in training. That's enough, but that's not a lot to compete with these people you need to compete with" in the stakes for high-quality horses.

In dividing the Claiborne horses between the racing stable and the sale, Hancock said, "We sent 13 yearlings to Holly Hill [training center] the other day, and we've got probably 20 in the sale" at Keeneland September in 2004.

And he is facing the same difficulty that his father did in trying to balance the confidence of buyers and retain a few horses for racing. He said, "I took the best colt we had to Keeneland last year – it was Stroll's full brother – and I couldn't get anybody to bid on him. We've got some nice horses going up there this year that I hope we can get people to bid on. But if they don't, that's fine. I'll take them to Holly Hill, too."

The yearlings that Claiborne took to the Keeneland sales in 2004 did well. The colt that Hancock pointed out as the best of the lot, a Danzig out of the Forty Niner mare Scads and a half-brother to the stakes filly Plenty, brought $2 million from Demi O'Byrne, buying for Coolmore and its associates.

In addition to marketing part of Claiborne's yearling crop, Hancock also has kept open other options for the farm. Claiborne and

Adele Dilschneider own mares in partnership, and "she doesn't want to sell anything. We've got 20 mares with her and 38 of our own. Of our 38, we'll keep some fillies, but we'll sell most all the colts. We did send two colts of our own to Holly Hill. One of them's a Danzig out of a mare called Watch the Time, who's been a wonderful mare for us. But he's a late May foal, and I thought, for one, I don't want to sell him, and two, I doubt we could get all that much for him.

"He is small, but he won't be for long. He's going to grow. He'll be fine. But a lot of buyers don't see that. They only see what they see right there in front of them."

## Into the Future

With the challenges of increasing commercialization of the market and breeding to capitalize on that, the fragmentation and greater competitiveness of stallion farms for essentially the same stallions, and the uncertainties of the purse structure in racing that is needed to give owners a reasonable shot at making back the money they put into horses, Claiborne and the Hancock family look into a future that is neither simple nor easily predictable.

They have a great history, and they take a positive view that there are great things ahead. Among the reasons for optimism about their operation and the future of the sport is the perspective the Hancocks have taken over the past century of racing.

Racing journalist, historian, and executive Timothy Capps assessed the farm and the men who made it this way: "Claiborne has stood for what a breeding operation would be if you could make it that way. They were straightforward, didn't get crazy one direction or another, took risks in a calculated manner, didn't jump on fads, had a long-term perspective. And I think that is what Seth has continued to do. And Arthur, too, in a somewhat different sphere. It's a hundred and some years they've been doing this, and they've taken an internationally prominent position because they've taken the long-term view. They treated clients the same, one price for all, and they are straight shooters.

"That's one of the reasons they've kept the clients they have over the years. They know that there are decisions to make and they will turn out to be wrong part of the time. But you don't want to feel that you're being led around and not all the hands are on the table.

"They've gone through a lot of eras. From the period of private stallions, to small ownerships, to stallion syndications, and into the modern day of huge books. But they've always been able to find the big horse without sacrificing their principles and still work in the best interest of their clients. I appreciate the way they do things. They're conservative and professional. It's the way you keep clients, way you keep people in the business for the long term. I wish everybody thought that way.

"They have succeeded in that they have taken the long view. We all get fooled about the potential of stallions, but they do business with the idea that they are in it for the long haul. This is the only sport in which pedigrees matter, and the legacy aspect of breeding is an important consideration. It is a vital part of why people get involved, and when you are thinking long term, you have to develop a sense of history and proportion. You can't get too carried away in what might be but have to plan for the best, whether it comes or not."

CHAPTER FOUR

# Arthur Hancock III: A New Path

In a history of the Hancocks, similarity is usually more commented on than difference. But each man, in each generation, has done some things differently, made his own mark, and established a sense of his own identity in the breeding of Thoroughbreds.

The elder Arthur Hancock, in partnership with his father, developed the first long-lasting commercial breeding operation for Thoroughbreds on a large-scale in the 20th century. Through the power of his personality and his skills at breeding and selecting good racehorses, the first Arthur Hancock became an immensely successful breeder.

Shortly after the mid-century, his son Bull moved away from the massive commercial approach. The second Arthur Hancock would never have advertised himself as a master salesman. To the contrary, his real love of the sport lay in racing, and as a result of the changes he made at Claiborne, Hancock became a leading owner-breeder and made Claiborne the premier stallion farm in the world.

Just as their father and grandfather before them had done, Seth Hancock and Arthur Hancock III have taken their own paths, each combining sales and racing as a means of working with the best stock and breeding the best horses. It's the family heritage.

But each generation faces a new challenge, has to learn from the past and adapt it to the present.

After growing up on Claiborne, Arthur Hancock went to college and then began his further education by going to the racetrack.

Hancock said, "I worked a year with Mr. Phipps' stable when I got out of Vanderbilt, year of '66, and I used to handle Buckpasser after the big races. I'd hot walk him, and man, he'd jump four feet off the ground, straight up in the air. Mr. [Eddie] Neloy [the Phippses' private trainer] had me handle Buckpasser because I had handled yearlings at Claiborne, was a good man, weighed 200 pounds, could bench press 300 pounds. I was good, but it used to make me nervous because, boy, he would jump."

The year of 1966 that marked Hancock's racetrack experience was an exceptional year, even for the Phipps family, as their stable had Bold Lad in his final season of racing, the champions Buckpasser, Successor, and Impressive, the high-class fillies Queen Empress, Destro, and Marking Time, as well as solid racers like Poker, Great Power, and Stupendous.

Despite the opportunity to catch the training bug in such exciting circumstances, Hancock said, "I liked the life on the farm. I did train a few after my dad died. I trained at Keeneland, and if they started out running for $30,000, in a month or two, they'd be running for $10,000. I couldn't train. There's an art to training. I just didn't have it, really.

"I liked the racetrack the year I was there. We had Buckpasser, Bold Lad (he was hurt by the time I got there), Successor, Queen Empress, and Marking Time.

"John Campo was the foreman, and he was a hell of a foreman, too. He couldn't understand what I was doing there, being a Hancock and working there, being there at six o'clock in the morning. He wouldn't give me a day off for about six months. He thought I was a spy for the Phipps family."

Despite Campo's suspicions about Hancock's presence at the stable, the grooms and hotwalkers seemed to have fun. Hancock recalled "that Dinny Phipps had four or five ducks there, and someone got them. I think I know who did it, a couple of guys from another barn down the road, but I spread the rumor around that Campo ate Dinny's ducks. We had a lot of fun."

After working on the racetrack for a year, Hancock "came back to Claiborne and worked there until 1970," he said. Then, "my dad said when he was my age, his father sent him to Virginia to run Ellerslie and told him, 'If you make it pay, I'll hire you back. If you can't, I don't need you.' He went out there to Virginia and made Ellerslie pay.

"Daddy leased a hundred acres to me and said, 'Do the same thing.'

"And he gave me four or five mares to keep, and then I got two or three other mares. I did that, and after a couple of years – he died in '72, in September – and I went back to Claiborne for three months until December. Then I came out on my own."

With this situation in mind, Seth Hancock said of his brother's work at Stone Farm: "His story, in my view, is more unique than this one [at Claiborne]. I've always thought that it was a hell of a lot tougher to take nothing and build it into something, and that's what he's done.

"If you take over managing the New York Yankees, you're supposed to win world championships. And that's what I did, took over managing the New York Yankees. And he took over managing the Montreal Expos, and he made it into a world champion."

In 1970, Bull Hancock leased 100 acres of Stone Farm to Arthur and sent him a few of Joseph Roebling's mares. In addition, "I had two of my own," he said. "I had bought Punctilious at the Keeneland November sale for $13,500. I actually bought her on the advice of my father, who said she was a nice mare." Punctilious, a foal of 1954, was a daughter of Better Self from the Bull Lea mare Puccoon and had produced the stakes winner Subtle (by Princequillo).

Being in foal was a major bonus to the value of Punctilious because she had a produce record that was littered with empty years. But she was in foal, and Forli was a promising young stallion who had been a great champion in South America and who had shown lots of speed in his brief racing career in North America.

Arthur Hancock bought the mare in 1969, and "The Pruner came along the year after," winning the American Derby in 1970 and running in the money for the Gulfstream Park Handicap and Donn Handicap the following year.

Although the mare died from complications of foaling in 1970, getting a foal from Punctilious was a great coup for Hancock because the mare's last foal was Dapper, who became a stakes winner in Ireland with trainer Vincent O'Brien.

When Dapper was a yearling, he caught the eye of the veteran Irish trainer, who suggested he could take the colt to Ireland and could probably sell a half-interest in him. And in fact, Charles St. George bought half the Forli colt for $25,000, which wasn't a bad sale for a young horse breeder in the early 1970s.

Better things were to come because the Forli colt named Dapper was Arthur's first stakes winner, and he put the young breeder on the road to success. Stakes-placed at two, Dapper won the Gladness and Tetrarch Stakes at three, and Arthur sold his remaining interest for a total of $190,000. With the money he made from selling Dapper, Hancock made the down payment on another 250 acres for Stone Farm.

## Striking Out on His Own

Bold Reasoning, a stallion who has had a lasting effect on the breed, especially as the sire of Seattle Slew, was a key element in the series of decisions that led Arthur Hancock to leave Claiborne and go his own way in the breeding business.

Hancock recalled, "Bunker Hunt was there at Claiborne with a lot of mares, and I was a friend of Bunker. And he called, Mr. Phipps was actually there on the farm, and he [Hunt] said, 'Arthur, I'd like to syndicate this horse into 33 shares and keep a third, which would be 11.' And I said, 'Well, that's all right.'

"I went back in, and they were having lunch at that time. I told them what Bunker had said, and Mr. Phipps said, 'Absolutely not. Every stallion at Claiborne is going to be syndicated into 32 shares.' And here I had told Bunker Hunt, who had more mares there at the time than Mr. Phipps did, frankly, . . .'" that syndicating the horse into a slightly atypical number of shares was all right. Now the farm advisers were telling Hancock that was not all right.

"That's what he [Phipps] said, though. And I thought to myself, . . . well, I just can't live like this."

Hancock was chafing under the conditions imposed by his father's will. Nor did it help his state of mind that his thoughts were being contradicted by Ogden Phipps and William Haggin Perry, two of the principal advisers appointed under the will. Hancock said, "Mr. Perry was another big client, and they were the two advisers, and Mr. Perry was always trying to tell me . . . like when we had this dispersal [of the Claiborne racing stable], I wanted to sell these horses at Keeneland, and my father would have rolled over in his grave to know they'd been sold at another company besides Keeneland. So right in the middle of this big meeting, I went and called George Swinebroad, and I said, 'Can we still sell these horses at the November sale?' And he said, 'We'll make a special catalog and put you right in the middle of it.'

"So I went back in the meeting and told them, and Mr. Perry said I was a hothead for having done that. Really pissed me off.

"And then this other thing came up with Mr. Phipps about Bold Reasoning. I had to call Bunker Hunt back and tell him that we can only do 32 shares at Claiborne. There's a long pause, and then he said, 'Well, that'll be all right, Arthur. I'll just keep nine or 10.' "

Repeatedly, as Arthur Hancock was making decisions about Claiborne and its operations, he was finding himself contradicted by the advisers.

He recalled that Stanley Gumberg, a longtime breeder and the owner of Skara Glen Stable, had visited Claiborne and the Hancocks in the late 1960s. Afterwards, Hancock said, "Daddy told me he thought Stanley Gumberg 'would make you boys a good client' if he wasn't there to look after things."

Gumberg kept a few mares at Claiborne, and Hancock recalled that soon "after Daddy had died, Mr. Gumberg wanted to breed two mares to Round Table. To me, that seemed all right because we wanted to establish good, new clients. But all hell broke loose about that. Mr. Phipps was mad that I was ready to give Mr. Gumberg two seasons. So I couldn't do what I wanted to do, even with someone who was a good man and a potential top client."

Bull Hancock had set up Claiborne to run like a corporation, not just an incorporated farm. It was to have the system of checks and balances similar to government, with the people concerned talking over every point and weighing the positives and negatives associated with each option.

Unfortunately, his elder son was not suited to the committee-style way of doing business, even though its deliberate and consensus-building approach to managing the farm was doubtless designed to safeguard the farm and eliminate as many risks as possible in its operation.

For Arthur Hancock, this was hell. It made him angry. It generally frustrated him and made him unhappy. But he was able to understand that the situation was not for him, despite his allegiance and connections to Claiborne.

So he left.

Hancock said, "There was a song called 'The Garden Party,' that Ricky Nelson had out that went, 'It's all right now. I've learned my lesson well. You see you can't please everyone. So you got to please yourself.'

"There's a line in it that says, 'If memories are all I send, I'd rather drive a truck.' And that's the way I am. I'd rather drive a semi from here to LA than to have to listen to that crap. Tell me how I'm going live my life, run my life.

"Not too many people know that Bold Reasoning was the straw that broke the camel's back in a way."

Arthur concurred with his brother that, had their father addressed the family about what he was doing exactly and why he was doing it and how he wanted it to work, it would have been better for all of them.

He said, "Yes, it probably would have been. But he died so suddenly. And the way it was left, there were three executors and three advisers. The advisers were Phipps and Perry and Charlie Kenny. And the executors were First Security Bank, Doug Parrish, and Sam Clay.

The executors were supposed to make their decisions based on the advice of the advisers, and two of the advisers were two of Claiborne's biggest clients, Mr. Phipps and Mr. Perry.

"And at the time, there was another thing involved. Seth was married and settled down. They wanted Seth to run Claiborne. I could see the writing on the wall. I told the executors at that meeting, you're supposed to follow the advice of the advisers, and I said, 'That's fine. Let Seth be the president,' but I was the oldest son, and I was hurt.

"And all this other stuff: about Bold Reasoning, the deal with Mr. Perry. I didn't like the whole feel of it. I wanted to see what I could do on my own. So I told the executors to follow the advice of the advisers, but I'm going to leave. I'm resigning.

"Oh no, they didn't want me to do that. My mother didn't want me to. But I did.

"That was the night I went down to Hall's and met my friend Paul Sullivan, and I got to drinking beer. I was real upset. In fact, I had tears coming down my face when I was going up and down the road out at Claiborne. I was drinking this Budweiser.

"I said, 'Sullivan, . . .

"He said, 'Arthur, all you want to do is drink, play that fucking guitar, and chase women. You don't want to work or anything.'

"I said, 'Paul, I really do, and I'm gonna tell you something: One of these days, I'm gonna win the Kentucky Derby and be bigger than Claiborne.'

"He said, 'Waitress, bring this fool another Budweiser.'

"And this was my best friend. He really meant it. He was just sad. He thought I was going to the dogs. And I did that. Became the first Hancock to win the Kentucky Derby. At one time, I had 4,600 acres, got bigger than Claiborne, got land poor, and owed all that money.

"Thank God I'm not bigger any more."

The third Arthur Hancock's decision to go his own way was not greeted with universal cheers. Some people envied him; others thought he was loco; and some were concerned for him. A young man can get into a lot of trouble on his own.

Without the framework of family, the structure of an established operation, and the advice of people who had been in the business for decades, many expected Hancock to spin out of control.

It is probably better not to overdo the psychology of the plan, but Bull Hancock had made provisions for anyone who wanted to opt out of the guidelines of his will. So, with $3.5 million from his share of the family trust established under the will, Arthur wasn't shoved out into the cold night. On the other hand, he didn't take the money, move to Barbados, and live off the interest. He set out to become the best horse breeder possible. Clearly, leaving Claiborne had to be a tough decision. When is a change and challenge of that sort easy?

Going on his own held risks and rewards for Hancock, and they were different ones than he would have had at Claiborne.

Establishing his own operation, without the restrictions that chafed him, seems to have been the best path. Hancock was able to march to his own drumbeat, focus on matters as he saw fit, and be in control of his own destiny.

Looking backward, it is undeniable that Hancock made an unqualified success of raising racehorses and making a living in the horse business, and he did it the way he thought was most fitting.

And from the first, some people responded positively to Hancock's decision. Perhaps they felt he was more in tune with them and their way of working than if he had stayed under the banner of Claiborne.

Not long after he struck out on his own, trainer Tommy Pratt called from California to ask Hancock if he would take a horse Pratt had been training for Leone Peters and stand him at Stone Farm. The horse was Cabin, a stakes-placed son of Bagdad from a grand family, and Peters had purchased the colt out of the Claiborne racing stable's dispersal following Bull Hancock's death. Arthur agreed to take the horse and syndicated him for $2,500 a share.

Courtesy Stone Farm

Arthur Hancock and Leone Peters

From their association through Cabin, Hancock and Peters became partners in some very good horses, and Peters became one of Stone Farm's most successful clients, with more than three dozen mares there at times. One of the greatest successes for Hancock and Peters resulted from a trip to Saratoga to buy yearlings.

The year after leaving Claiborne, Hancock went to the Saratoga sale and bought a Jacinto yearling filly for $20,000. As a breeding man would, Hancock noted that the filly had a pedigree built on the same pattern as Bold Reasoning, by a son of Bold Ruler and out of a daughter of Hail to Reason.

Furthermore, the filly was a gray, and Hancock said, "I figured she must have inherited some of the genes from her third dam, Silver Fog, who had produced Silver Spoon, The Searcher, Silver Bright, and Silver True."

This was one of the great C.V. Whitney families, and Hancock's filly traced back through one of the lesser daughters of Silver Fog, Yellow Mist (by Hierocles), and the Hail to Reason dam was a non-winner. This appeared to be no better than an average branch of a nice family, but Hancock had selected a good runner.

He brought in Peters to be his partner, and they raced the filly in California. Named Peacefully, the gray filly won the Luther Burbank Stakes and was second in the Torrey Pines.

The best foal out of the Hail to Reason mare Morning Calm, Peacefully was retired to stud after her racing career proved a success, and she was sent to Stone Farm's best stallion at the time, the great Chilean-bred distance runner Cougar.

Cougar was champion turf horse in 1972, but the 'Big Cat' wasn't just good on turf. He was good at a distance. He could finish, and he was dead game, no matter what the weight. Trained by Charlie Whittingham, Cougar showed what he was made of – and what Whittingham could do with a loaded gun – when the horse won the Santa Anita Handicap off works alone in 1973.

But in the general consensus of the commercial marketplace, there was no way you could make Cougar seem like a fashionable sire of early-maturing, quick horses. After standing his first two seasons at the Spendthrift Farm of Leslie Combs, Cougar was in commercial trouble.

For most horses, that spells the end of the line. Cougar, however, had an owner who believed in him.

Mary Bradley, who initially had owned the horse in partnership with Charlie Whittingham and then without him, asked Arthur Hancock if he could syndicate Cougar for $30,000 per share and stand him for $10,000.

Perhaps someone more bitterly accustomed to the mishaps of the marketplace would not have undertaken the challenge, but Hancock decided to make it work. Bradley kept 14 shares in the stallion; Arthur sold 22.

Even with that much success, the going wasn't easy. Bradley "had only about six mares to go to Cougar," Hancock recalled. "I had to sell her other seasons and the 22 shares, and it took me about four months to get that done."

Hancock said, "Cougar was the first major syndication I completed on my own" in the spring of 1976. It would not be the last.

In the stallion's first season at Stone, Cougar had 40 mares, and his fee had risen to $20,000 by 1982, the year that Gato del Sol won the Kentucky Derby for Hancock and Peters.

Since Cougar was his best stallion and Peacefully was a stakes winner, Hancock and Peters sent their young mare to the 'Big Cat.'

Their first offspring was a filly named Tasha Two, and the second was Gato del Sol.

Stone Farm retained only two yearlings from its 1979 crop of foals, and the gray colt named Gato del Sol was one of them.

Courtesy Stone Farm

Arthur Hancock and Charlie Whittingham with Gato Del Sol.

A good-class two-year-old, Gato del Sol had closed from far back to win the Del Mar Futurity as a juvenile and was among the dozen highest-rated colts on the Experimental Free Handicap of 1981.

Although he didn't win with great consistency, Gato del Sol had gameness and ability, even though his racing style was somewhat contradictory for American racing, which places a premium on speed and maneuverability. In contrast, Cougar and his son had a long, rather loping sort of stride with a fair bit of knee action.

Whittingham reminded the colt's trainer, Eddie Gregson, of this similarity, and Gregson said at the time, "This influenced me even more to have the rider give him time to get into his stride."

131

Prior to the 1982 Kentucky Derby, Gato del Sol had shown his ability to finish in the San Felipe, Santa Anita Derby, and Blue Grass, though without winning any of them.

In the Derby, jockey Eddie Delahoussaye followed his riding orders. He let Gato del Sol find his best stride, which meant that the colt dawdled along at the back of the pack of 19 racers till past the half-mile pole.

Moving from 19th at the half to seventh at the three-quarters, Gato del Sol had found his best stride and was only three and a half lengths off the leaders in fourth after a mile. The gray kept slugging all the way down the stretch at Churchill Downs, and he pulled away from Reinvested to win by two and a half lengths.

In minutes, Hancock was standing in the winner's circle at Churchill Downs with his first Kentucky Derby winner, Gato del Sol, whom he bred, owned, and raced in partnership with Leone J. Peters. Less than a decade after leaving Claiborne, Hancock had accomplished one of the most difficult of the goals he set for himself on his path to success.

By 1982, Stone Farm had grown from 100 acres and five mares into 2,500 acres, 210 broodmares, nine stallions, and "a cast of thousands," as the movie producers might say. Hancock had developed his little patch into a large and thriving breeding operation that was succeeding at the classic level and bringing in major clients. It was an immense accomplishment that required enormous reserves of cash and energy to sustain. At the most elemental level, there was a lot of grass to mow on that much land.

A large part of Hancock's approach to expansion was organized around acquiring and managing stallions. To play at the top of the game, however, he knew that quality was more important than quantity. The fall after syndicating Cougar, Hancock had the chance to pursue even bigger game in stallion acquisition.

That year Aaron Jones had consolidated all his broodmares onto the Stone Farm operation, and he called Hancock in the fall of 1976 and asked him whether Kentucky Derby winner Bold Forbes would be a good buy as a stallion prospect at $4 million.

Hancock's answer was "yes" and really quick.

Not just every stallion manager would have been so bold. A freakishly fast horse, Bold Forbes had led every step of the Kentucky Derby and vanquished the odds-on favorite Honest Pleasure. Then two weeks later in the Preakness, Honest Pleasure and Bold Forbes hooked up on the lead, ran each other into defeat, and finished well behind the winner, Elocutionist.

For the Belmont three weeks later, Laz Barrera regrouped. He gave his dark brown colt long gallops, encouraging the colt to relax and make the most of his natural talent. In the race, Bold Forbes winged away into a long lead and just lasted to win the mile and a half race through his own gameness and the riding enterprise of Angel Cordero, who would rather be on the lead than be president.

Bold Forbes had cut a hoof during the Belmont, however, and missed most of the rest of the year.

A winner of seven consecutive races at two, Bold Forbes was amazingly quick. He was also small and not very impressive to some observers.

Bold Forbes was a first-rate racehorse, however, and Hancock was eager to undertake the challenge of standing a horse with his level of ability. In part because the commercial breeders of racehorses had some reservations about Bold Forbes' prospects as a sire, Hancock did not finalize the Bold Forbes syndication until the following spring.

Pricing shares in the horse at $130,000, Jones kept 10 shares, swapped another 10 to Bunker Hunt for interests in some of the young Hunt stallions, and sold the 16 other shares after Hunt announced he would breed his international champion Dahlia to Bold Forbes.

The same fall that he began work on the Bold Forbes syndication, Hancock also sold a Hawaii yearling colt for $32,000 to Robert Sangster. Named Hawaiian Sound, the colt ran second in the English Derby in 1978 and became a Group 1 stakes winner in England. Hancock had reacquired an interest in the colt, along with Peters, and eventually stood Hawaiian Sound at Stone.

Hancock and Peters bred and raced a Riva Ridge colt named Tap Shoes, who won the Hopeful and Futurity at two, as well as the Flamingo at three, but he did not succeed in their highest goal, the Kentucky Derby. Their second try was with Gato del Sol.

# Making Stallions

In between Hancock's first Derby and his second, he moved further along the path of making Stone Farm a significant operation by standing world-class stallions. Stone had a couple of younger sires in residence, including classic winner Bold Forbes, with indications of sound success, but none had risen to the rank of leading sire.

The farm needed a cornerstone stallion, one who would bring highest-quality mares in significant numbers to the farm. Of the many benefits that having a premium-level stallion brings to a farm, there is not only the business he generates and the income and prestige that result from his offspring but also the added lift a top stallion gives to the other horses around him.

To acquire such a horse requires either extreme good fortune or a great deal of cash. Both elements combined in Hancock's association with breeder and financier Tom Tatham, who entered the horse business in the early 1980s and created numerous partnerships for investors in Thoroughbreds.

Initially, Tatham bought high-end broodmares and broodmare prospects, put them into partnerships under the Oak Cliff banner for wealthy investors, and sold the resulting foals at auction. This approach worked well, especially in the early 1980s, and Tatham decided he would like to expand his investments into stallions, as well.

And so it was that Hancock's connection with breeder-investor Tom Tatham brought a stallion to the farm who was the nation's leader. His name was Halo.

In early 1984, after Sunny's Halo had won the previous year's Kentucky Derby and Devil's Bag had been named champion two-year-old colt of 1983 off an impressive unbeaten season and had been syndicated for more than $34 million, Tatham offered to purchase shares in Halo for $900,000 apiece. The leading sire in North America in 1983, Halo was a really good stallion but was naturally second banana (or maybe third) on the Windfields Farm roster, which was led by the great Northern Dancer.

With his lucrative offer, Tatham snapped up 27 of the syndicate's 40 shares, and he moved the stallion to Kentucky to stand at Stone Farm.

A $100,000 select sale yearling, Halo had a splendid pedigree, being a son of champion juvenile Hail to Reason (by former Claiborne stallion Turn-to) out of the important broodmare Cosmah. The mare produced champion Tosmah and the stakes winner Maribeau before she was sold to John Gaines. She foaled the good sales yearlings and stakes winners Fathers Image and Halo for Gaines, as well as the Ribot mare Queen Sucree, who produced Kentucky Derby winner Cannonade.

As this indicates, Halo had all the genetic substance to be a grand sire. All he had to do was prove his worth as a racehorse. And he did.

Although his pedigree showed plenty of speed and early maturity, both from his sire and his female family, Halo was really something of a late bloomer. After he had run third in important races like the Dwyer, Jersey Derby, and Jim Dandy, Halo broke through and won the Lawrence Realization, run on turf at a mile and a half.

Presently, scarcely any farm would even stand a stallion that won 12-furlong stakes on turf. It is mistakenly presumed the kiss of death.

Halo raced on and won the United Nations and Tidal Handicap, both good races on turf. And neither is a sprint.

Retired to stud initially at Windfields Farm in Maryland, Halo was a success from the first. Not surprisingly, almost all his offspring were best at a mile or more. And in 1983, the stallion broke into the elite ranks of international sires. He sired the winner of the Kentucky Derby, Sunny's Halo, and his son Devil's Bag was an unbeaten juvenile champion.

A medium-sized dark brown horse, Halo was a more neatly made horse than his rangy sire, taking after some of the elements in his female family, such as the English Derby winner Mahmoud, who had speed and stamina.

Halo, like both Mahmoud and Hail to Reason, sired racehorses who had speed and could carry it reasonable distances. Adding him to the stallion roster at Stone Farm moved the operation forward several steps in public recognition and in the capacity to produce classic racehorses.

But all is not easy, even with leading sires. As with a good stallion on any farm, Windfields wasn't thrilled to see Halo leave, but not many shed tears to see him go, either. Halo, you see, was a horse who could be tough.

In fact, in *The Blood-Horse* of May 13, 1989, Dede Biles quoted Charlie Whittingham describing the personalities of Halo and some of his stock: "Halo is a pretty mean sucker, and he'll tear you apart. All his sons and daughters are a little that way. Sunday Silence is very fiery, and he'll grab you in a minute, but he's not really mean. [Kentucky Oaks winner] Goodbye Halo is a little cranky, and she'll kick the brains out of you. [Grade 1 winner] Lively One is the nicest."

Being sweet isn't always the best sign in a racehorse. Whittingham, for instance, attributed the desire to race hard and win to the Halos' fiery natures.

## Back to the Derby

One of the credos that Arthur Hancock lives by is that "raising good horses is an art." Love them or not, the Hancocks have learned something about raising horses over the years, and the results at the racetracks of the world bear out their confidence in well-tried methods.

As an owner rather than the breeder, Arthur Hancock won the Kentucky Derby for the second time in 1989 with the near-black colt Sunday Silence, by Stone Farm stallion Halo. This horse and his extraordinary history from foal to Derby winner is perhaps more exceptional than even that of Seabiscuit, who was raised at Claiborne for the Wheatley Stable of Gladys Mills Phipps.

Although he stood the sire and raised the son, Sunday Silence wasn't bred by Hancock. Sunday Silence was bred by Tom Tatham's Oak

Cliff Thoroughbreds. And although Oak Cliff raced some horses, it was primarily structured as a breeding and sales operation.

At that time, Hancock said, "Tom Tatham had Ted Keefer from Texas as his adviser, and he'd come in here every month and check on things. He'd been a racetrack vet and knew something about racetracks and legs. Didn't know a damned thing about foals or anything. So he started coming in here. He'd come in being something like Napoleon, all reared back, and start telling us all these things to do with feet and everything. We already had the best blacksmith around."

But Keefer, whom Hancock calls a "good and sensible guy," also offered his input into the prospects and management of the Oak Cliff stock.

Hancock continued, "When Sunday Silence was a yearling, I remember him [Keefer] looking at him, and he'd say, 'Put that black sonofabitch back in there.' Every time, he'd say, 'I don't even want to see him.' "Every time, he'd say that. So he came another time, and they brought Sunday Silence out, who was called the Wishing Well colt [at that time]. And he said, 'Oh, I know what that bastard looks like.'

"Pete Logan was the farm manager, and one day he said, 'Mr. Keefer, he'd look mighty good with the roses around his neck,' like country boys will joke around. Keefer said, 'The only time that sonofabitch will have a rose around his neck is when he's under ground.' "And that was Sunday Silence," who went on to win not only the Kentucky Derby but the Preakness and Breeders' Cup Classic.

Like many another professional, Hancock has pride in his work and a sense of dignity about how it is done. Not surprisingly, he resented the assistance he hadn't asked for. Keefer "was coming in here, dictating to us, to me, how I was going to run my farm. I have to work and do my best, and I finally told Tom, and he had about 25 mares here, 'Let's just stay friends; just move your mares. Ted Keefer is not going to run Stone Farm. I am.'

"And so he moved the mares. Now, the mares are back. Tom and I are friends. Of course, Sunday Silence came up after that, and Keefer looked like an idiot. Well, none of us know about a horse. Ted is a hard worker, a good horseman, and he was out of his league when he was coming up here. People who have been in this business for generations know something about a horse, about foals. Again, though, if you're going to make it in this world, this business, you can't have someone dictating to you."

By standing his ground and saying what he thought, Hancock lost an account in the short term, regained it in the long term, and kept his composure about a trying situation. As a result, he said, "Tom and I are friends, and I've got a yearling in the 2004 Saratoga sales for him, an Unbridled's Song colt."

Also as part of his relationship with Tatham, and in the most round about way imaginable, Hancock got the horse of a lifetime. He bought Sunday Silence.

As agent for Oak Cliff, Hancock consigned Sunday Silence to the Keeneland July yearling sale in 1987, and "I bought him back out of our consignment for $17,000. I gave Tom the ticket, and I said, 'I bought him back for you. He was too cheap.'

"He said, 'We don't want him because Ted doesn't like him.' And I said, 'OK,' and I remember this like I'm sitting and talking to you. I had a shirt on with a pocket in it, and I stuck the ticket in the pocket and thought, 'Well, guess I just blew another $17,000.' "That's when I owed all that money and had all that debt. And that's what I thought.

Sunday Silence with his groom

Courtesy Stone Farm

"That was Sunday Silence: A gift from God."

At the time, however, the colt didn't seem like much of a gift at all. Hancock took his new acquisition back to Stone, broke the colt, tried to sell him as a two-year-old in training, and being unwilling to sell the colt cheaply, nearly lost him when the van hauling the young horse back to Kentucky had a wreck. Given time to recuperate, Sunday Silence was fine after all and eventually went to trainer Charlie Whittingham, who had trained Cougar. Whittingham took a half-interest in Sunday Silence and then sold half of his part to Dr. Ernest Gaillard.

The dark colt progressed nicely at two, then went unbeaten through the spring of his three-year-old season, winning the classic preps on the West Coast, including the Santa Anita Derby. Then on a cold and blustery Kentucky afternoon, he won the Kentucky Derby for Hancock and partners, defeating the favored Easy Goer.

When the two met again 14 days later in the Preakness, the weather was better, the race was even more exciting, and the outcome was much closer. In one of the best classic races ever, Easy Goer made a dramatic move from the half, when he was running fifth, to be first at the three-quarters. In the process, the chestnut son of Alydar passed Sunday Silence, who had been running third.

Then Sunday Silence made a dramatic move of his own, accelerating around the turn to draw even with his rival before reaching the mile. From there to the wire, the black and the red raced head to head. At one point, Sunday Silence put a neck in front of Easy Goer, who again drew even. A sixteenth from the wire, Easy Goer took a narrow lead. Again, the nimble son of Halo was able to overtake his opponent and won the race by a nose.

Now Hancock and his partners were not simply proud winners of the Kentucky Derby. They had succeeded in winning the first two races in the Triple Crown, and one more victory would write an amazing page of racing history for them and the young dark horse that nobody liked except Hancock and Whittingham.

In the Belmont, however, Easy Goer ran his best race of the Triple Crown, and Ogden Phipps' best horse since Buckpasser became his owner's first American classic winner. After late summer successes for

Arthur Hancock and Charlie Whittingham

both colts, they met for the fourth and last time in the Breeders' Cup Classic. The agility and push-button acceleration of Sunday Silence allowed him to win the archrivals' final encounter, and as a result, he earned he Eclipse Awards as both champion three-year-old and Horse of the Year.

As a four-year-old, Sunday Silence had an abbreviated season of racing before an injury forced his retirement. In a perfect world, Sunday Silence would then have come home to Stone Farm, been syndicated for the large sums typically paid for top-flight champions, and become part of the Stone Farm story as a stallion.

But this wasn't a perfect world. Thoroughbred breeding was in the pit of the bloodstock depression brought on by speculation and the tax law changes of the late 1980s.

When Hancock tried to syndicate Sunday Silence, he couldn't get it done. He said, "Here I was with the Horse of the Year, and I couldn't sell a half-dozen shares. Only Warner Jones, Josephine Abercrombie, and one or two others were willing to show their confidence in the horse."

A few others would likely have bought seasons to the horse in his first year at stud, but Hancock was assessing the realities of his situation and it was not pretty.

As part of his ambition to expand Stone Farm and make it bigger than Claiborne, he had acquired parcel after parcel of land. Now he was land poor, and the collapse in horse prices at the sales was making him horse poor, as well.

When the situation was looking bleak, Zenya Yoshida, who had purchased a quarter-interest in Sunday Silence earlier in the year for $2.5 million, offered to buy out all the partners for a sum greater than what the Kentucky Derby and Preakness winner was likely to earn in many years of stud fees, approximately another $8.5 million.

"It just killed me to do it," Hancock said. "But what was I going to do? The other fellows weren't really into the breeding business, and I had all this debt staring at me. So we did the practical thing and took the money."

Selling Sunday Silence might have been the smartest move that Hancock ever made. The income from the horse's sale totalled more than $10 million to the three partners, and his portion of the sale cleared the decks for Stone Farm. Hancock was able to go forward with encumbrances, without so much worry, and plan for himself and his family.

For Yoshida, the purchase price was high, but Sunday Silence became the greatest sire in the history of Japanese breeding.

Courtesy Stone Farm

Teruya Yoshida with Arthur Hancock. Sunday Silence became the greatest sire in the history of Japanese breeding under the management of the Yoshida family.

Annually receiving the very best mares available from breeders in Japan, and there were some outstanding broodmares available there by the time that Sunday Silence went to stud, Sunday Silence became the leading sire in Japan. He set records for number of stakes winners, as well as stakes earnings, and his sons and daughters are having a significant impact on Japanese breeding.

Would the dark horse have been a major success if he had remained in Kentucky? With the state of the industry in 1990, he would have had to prove himself every step of the way.

# An Art and a Blessing

As Hancock went forward with his program at Stone Farm, the sale of Sunday Silence freed him from many of the concerns he had felt during that time. He had worked hard to develop the immense Stone Farm operation, had brought in clients who had assisted with the improvement in the farm's position and bloodstock, and had made a success of breeding and racing horses at the highest level.

In addition to the work ethic that his father instilled and that Arthur did not always show in his youth, he has become one of the world's consummate horsemen.

Seth gives his brother high praise. "Arthur has been very successful, and he's done it on his own." That element of independence is an essential part of Arthur's makeup.

As Arthur said to me when writing this book, "With owners and breeders, there has to be a mutual respect. I'll work for you, but don't tell me how to write my story. You're a writer; you know what I mean. Yeah, that's your thing. Sure, you get some tips from a good editor, but ...."

Nobody can write it for you.

On occasion, Hancock has had owners who wanted to write the story, and that hasn't worked out in the long term.

Just as his father had to part with the Guggenheim horses rather than surrender his principles, Arthur Hancock said, "I used to have Aaron Jones . . . had 25, 30 mares. We raised a lot of good horses for him: Tiffany Lass, all those other stakes winners by Bold Forbes . . . lot of great stakes winners that Laz [Barrera] trained. One year they told me to pick out the five worst yearlings and sell them. I told them I don't know who they are because the one I pick might turn out to be good."

In short, Hancock's advice was, "If you're gonna race 'em, just race 'em all." But Jones had "this one crooked colt by Exclusive Native, and Laz said, 'We ought to sell him, anyway.' And I said, 'Well, Harry Trotsek always said, "Send me the crooked ones." ' And he did."

The rationale in that statement is that a horse's raw conformation does not mean that a horse will be able to race successfully or not. Sometimes conformation will prevent a good horse from showing its ability, sometimes not. Conformation mostly counts at the sales, when advisers are trying to select horses by eliminating ones with potential defects.

So Hancock told Jones and his advisers, "Just race him, get him claimed. He's not going to bring anything at the sale, and you never know." He might be good enough to overcome apparent faults.

"So they kept them all," Hancock said, "and that colt turned out to be Valdez."

Barrera took his time with the leggy chestnut colt, gave him time to grow and harden his joints. Racing only at three and four, Valdez won half of his 16 starts, earning more than a half-million dollars for Jones. The chestnut son of Exclusive Native and the Graustark mare Sally Stark earned his most important victory in the Grade 1 Swaps Stakes.

Hancock recalled that "Lo and behold, Brownell Combs offered Aaron Jones $8 million for him. I said, 'Mr. Jones, I'd sell him.' I thought he should stand for about $15,000. At that time, that was $60,000 a share, with 40 shares, making him worth between $2 million and $2 and a half million.

"I told him to take it, and he did. And Valdez went over there to Spendthrift.

"It wasn't a year or two after that and this horse we raised and broke here wouldn't turn but one way in the stall. It was Lemhi Gold."

Lemhi Gold was good at three and became champion older horse at four, winning three Grade 1 races: the Jockey Club Gold Cup, the Marlboro Cup, and the San Juan Capistrano. At five, with the goal of making him Horse of the World, Jones and stallion investor John Gaines sent the chestnut son of Vaguely Noble to race in Europe.

Hancock told Jones, "Don't do that. You're going to have a champion, Horse of the Year. There's nothing to gain. Well, they ran him, and he got beat." In his three starts in Europe, Lemhi Gold wouldn't rate behind the European horses and was unplaced each time.

Hancock said, "About that same time, we had about 25 weanlings, just gorgeous. Mr. Jones had good mares, was a good student of pedigrees, and we raised some good horses here. But he had this vet, Joe Cannon, and Joe Cannon decided they had a farm in Oregon and they'd bring all these weanlings and raise them in Oregon.

"So they sent a damned semi-truck in here that had about three windows on each side, and they wanted to put all these weanlings in this truck together like a herd of cattle. And send them out to Oregon. I took pride in raising these horses, and our record was so good, what we raised for him. Seeing all these beautiful babies – we had to load them on this damned thing and send them out – really got to me. And I thought, I keep all these mares here, and I don't sell any yearlings, and you don't make any money boarding horses really."

Much as he had enjoyed working with Jones and having his stock on Stone Farm, Hancock was becoming uncomfortable with the working relationship. And the idea of treating Thoroughbreds, not like individuals or like horses but instead like cattle, was getting to him. He said, "And all this happened about the time Lemhi Gold came along. I didn't want to stand Lemhi Gold. He was by Vaguely Noble, and none of his sons had done any good, but still he was a beautiful horse, and I had a mare named Lullaby who was a stakes winner and a full sister to Hawaiian Sound. I told Mr. Jones that I'd like to breed Lullaby to Lemhi Gold. I think it'd be a good cross, and it's a good mare for the horse.

"I raised him and raised Valdez. 'What about a complimentary season?'

"I didn't stand the horse, but they got $8 million for him, $8 million for Valdez, and raised all these other good horses.

"He said, 'You'll pay like anybody else.'

"When he told me that, the same thing clicked in me that clicked in my father. I went up and saw Mr. Jones at the sales not long after, and

I said, 'The best thing to do is to move your mares.'

"I didn't want to see any more of those weanlings going out of here. I didn't want to raise him another good horse and not have a chance to stand him. Basically, I felt unappreciated. And I'm not going to work for somebody who doesn't appreciate me. So we parted company."

Once again in Hancock's life, a contradiction between the way he wanted to live his life and the way someone else wanted to live theirs caused a parting of the ways. It was a significant financial loss to a growing operation like Stone Farm, which had been a primary factor in the breeding program of Jones, as well as in others.

In a purely financial sense, it wasn't a pragmatic move. Hancock admitted, "Sometimes I think, 'Maybe I was stupid to do that.' But you know, if you're going to get up early and work around here seven days a week for these people, you need to be appreciated and need to like your job. If you don't, why go on?"

But for all the occasional differences that Hancock found in dealing with people, even more often he found that alliances built over time produced good fruit. From his lengthy association with Leone Peters, Hancock bred his second classic winner, the Secretariat horse Risen Star.

Risen Star was out of the His Majesty mare Ribbon, whom Hancock had purchased for himself and Peters. At the 1978 Keeneland fall yearling sale, Hancock had noticed a good-looking yearling filly by His Majesty out of the Hail to Reason mare Break Through. The filly was bred by John Galbreath, sold to Hancock for $28,000, was named Ribbon, and became a stakes winner at three for Hancock and Peters, earning more than 10 times her purchase price.

The mare's first two named foals were by the Stone Farm stallions Bold Forbes and Northern Baby. And before the partners bred their mare to another home stallion, an opportunity came their way. Trainer Lucien Laurin, who had a lifetime breeding right in Secretariat for training the great champion, wanted to breed a mare to Stone stallion Northern Baby, a young Northern Dancer horse who was a very good racehorse in Europe.

So Hancock swapped a season to Northern Baby for a season to Secretariat and then sent Ribbon to the Triple Crown winner.

The result was Risen Star.

In 1985, Peters had chosen to disperse his breeding stock, and Hancock consigned 40 horses to the Keeneland November sale. They grossed more than $4.5 million. Included in the group was the stakes-winning mare Ribbon, who had been a good mare for the Hancock and Peters partnership.

Her first foal, Premier Partner (by Bold Forbes), had shown some talent in 1985, winning four of his eight starts and placing third in the Grade 3 Fairmount Derby. So the partners had decided their young mare was going to be a serious producer and had stepped up their plans for her, sending her to the most popular young sire of the day.

As a result, Ribbon, in foal to leading sire Danzig, sold for $2 million to Darley Stud Management. At the time, Risen Star was a weanling. (Ribbon produced five named foals for Darley. Two were stakes winners, including the Danzig filly she was carrying at the time of the sale, who was named Silk Braid. A third filly was group stakes-placed.)

As Peters continued to disperse his Thoroughbred holdings, he also sold off Ribbon's foal of 1985 as a yearling. A big, growthy colt who was dark brown instead of his sire's gleaming chestnut, Risen Star was sent to the Keeneland July sale with a reserve of $250,000. Hancock bought the colt in at $210,000 and purchased his partner's half-interest in the colt.

Hancock resold the big, dark colt as a two-year-old in training at the 1987 Fasig-Tipton Calder sale of select juveniles, and Risen Star brought $300,000 from Louie Roussel.

A stakes winner at two from only three starts, Risen Star improved dramatically in the first half of 1988. Racing for the partnership of Roussel and Ron Lamarque, the leggy colt showed that he could stretch out and inhale his rivals through the stretch, winning prep races at the Fair Grounds for the Louisiana Derby.

Then he won the Louisiana Derby, beat Forty Niner in the Lexington Stakes at Keeneland, and finished third after a troubled trip in the Kentucky Derby.

The big colt won the final two races of his career, the Preakness and Belmont Stakes, in tremendous style and promised to be the closest that Secretariat ever came to reproducing a racer of his own exalted class.

The same year that Risen Star won classics for Roussel and Lamarque, Hancock won the Kentucky Oaks with a flashy chestnut filly named Goodbye Halo. Owned in partnership with Alex Campbell, Goodbye Halo was one of the very best daughters of Halo.

The partners acquired the talented chestnut, Hancock said, because "bloodstock adviser John Adger recommended that I buy Goodbye Halo from her owner, John Ballis. I believe I paid $700,000 for her, but it turned out to be a good purchase. She had just won the Demoiselle Stakes in New York when John told me that Ballis wanted to sell her, and he said she was a runner. I owed all that money, and she helped a lot (earning slightly more than $1.7 million) and turned out great. I'd never have bought her at all without John. He also introduced me to Tom Tatham and to the McNairs.

Bloodstock adviser John Adger with Arthur Hancock

A winner of seven Grade 1 stakes at two, three and four, Goodbye Halo earned more than $1.7 million.

Her pedigree reflected Hancock's appreciation for Claiborne sires, as Goodbye Halo was out of a mare by Sir Ivor, with the second dam by Buckpasser and the third dam by Princequillo.

In addition to sticking with patterns in bloodlines that had worked, Hancock also continues to race and breed horses in partnerships with people of similar interest and enthusiasm for the game. And in breeding his most recent classic winner, Hancock combined both premium Claiborne bloodlines and one of his most successful partnerships, which was formed several years ago with Robert and Janice McNair.

As the McNairs began to become active in Thoroughbred racing and breeding, they wanted to buy some broodmares. And Hancock's advice was to buy the best they could find. "Breeding the best to the best and hoping for the best" may sound like a simple dictum until it comes to acquiring the best. They usually are very expensive.

Having the McNairs as partners in purchasing broodmares made it easier to acquire better stock, and they began their program of improvement with the purchase of Angel Fever at the dispersal of the Loblolly Stable broodmares at the 1994 Keeneland November sale. A young, stakes-placed daughter of Danzig and the Halo mare Rowdy Angel, Angel Fever was a full sister to Preakness winner Pine Bluff and a half-sister to Kentucky Derby favorite Demons Begone. Carrying her second foal on a cover to Claiborne champion and sire Forty Niner, Angel Fever was a premium broodmare.

In fact, she was the kind of broodmare who usually hovered outside Hancock's grasp at the breeding stock sales. And he said, "I'll have to admit, without the McNairs, I wouldn't have been able to get a really nice young mare like Angel Fever."

As is typical with a mare of this quality, the bidding was strong. And Hancock was getting nervous. He said, "I hit her at $475,000, then someone came back at $500,000. I'd had about enough, but Bob (McNair), said, 'Let's try another one. If she's worth $500,000, she's worth another $25,000.' When you walk in the jungle and have the silverback gorilla beside you, it gives you a lot of confidence. So I bid again, and we got her."

And, simply as that, the partners bought themselves the dam of a Kentucky Derby winner.

After producing a filly by Forty Niner, the mare went back to that horse's sire, the grand old man of Claiborne Farm, Mr. Prospector. That mating resulted in a $1 million Keeneland July sale filly later named Blissful, but the mare saved her best for next, as her fourth foal was a grand-looking Mr. Prospector colt. The colt was so handsome and robust that he was nicknamed Superman at Stone Farm, where he was raised.

Hancock said, "Most of the time you can't really tell how a yearling is going to turn out. They can really fool you until they get out there and race, but with this colt, just like Risen Star, they really stood out."

So handsome and promising that Hancock tried to create partnerships to purchase a half-interest in the colt for $500,000 when he was a weanling. The Superman colt went to the 1998 Keeneland July sale and brought not one but four million dollars.

The successful bidder was John Ward, bidding for Japanese businessman Fusao Sekiguchi, and the colt was named Fusaichi Pegasus.

Fusaichi Pegasus, winner of the 2000 Kentucky Derby,
Kent Desormeaux up

Less than two years later, the super bay colt won the Kentucky Derby in 2000 and became the hottest stallion property in the world. The underbidders on him at the Keeneland sale had been a consortium of Coolmore and allies, and after the colt had proven himself, Coolmore came back to Sekiguchi as the successful bidder for breeding rights to Fusaichi Pegasus. Coolmore paid something more than $60 million for the breeding rights to Fusaichi Pegasus because he was such an outstanding athlete, was such an outstanding sales yearling, was by the greatest sire of stallions living, and was out of a full sister to another classic winner from a good old family.

The horse had all it takes to become an important stallion, perhaps a great one. And that consideration, even more than the profitability of racing a top horse, was Hancock's motive in trying to set up a partnership to retain the yearling later named Fusaichi Pegasus. He said, "As the business is now, I can't afford to buy top-end stallion prospects." The pricing on stallion prospects, particularly those at the top of market, is predicated on breeding them to books of more than 100 mares – actually a great deal more than 100 mares – and typically also shuttling them to the Southern Hemisphere, almost always Australia, so that they can be bred to more mares in the off season of the Northern Hemisphere and get more foals.

The price of large books falls hardest on breeders who use the most popular stallions yet end up with yearlings who attract few lookers or buyers. Hancock noted that "when people go up there and sell yearlings at an average of two times the stud fee, a few people make money, but most of them won't. I'm 61 now, and I hope to live some time longer. I'll keep doing what I'm doing" in avoiding the most heavily patronized stallions and standing his own horses to a limited number of mares.

With the intense competition that the mega-book has brought to the sales and stallion market, Hancock said, "I can't compete for stallions because I'm not going to breed them to huge books. So I can't compete economically for stallions. I'm going to race a few colts in hopes of getting a stallion that way," and Fusaichi Pegasus would certainly have been a tremendous coup had Hancock managed to retain a significant interest in him.

Although the prices paid for stallions such as Fusaichi Pegasus are difficult to comprehend for most of us, there is a philosophical and ethical question in the equation that bothers Hancock most.

He noted that his father believed that overbreeding a stallion "compromises the quality of his offspring." The question of overbreeding is a key criticism of the enormous books being covered by many stallions since the mid-1990s.

Taking his father's comment as a starting point in his own assessment, he said, "If that's true, then maybe the ones overbreeding will compromise themselves to the point that those of us not overusing the horses will come out OK. Horatio Luro said, 'Don't squeeze the lemon dry.' That goes for every aspect of the business. If you stay close to nature, God and nature will deliver a good horse."

Like many craftsmen or artists, Hancock can become philosophical when he comes to talk about raising horses.

Courtesy Stone Farm

Staci and Arthur Hancock with 1997 Broodmare of the Year Ann Campbell

In raising horses, Hancock said, "I believe in sticking as close to nature as possible. You have to have good land, and you have to keep it fresh. I rotate cattle onto fields, give fields two or three months rest in between. We're farmers, and the crop we raise is horses. If you take care of horses, the horses will take care of you."

Hancock's plain truth approach to horses has implications in all directions, however. While the suggestion about supplying "fresh air" is easy to come by in Kentucky, giving them "plenty of room to run" is more of a challenge as industrial development and encroachment from subdivisions becomes more common.

He also believes that Thoroughbreds should not be given too much pampering. "Don't hothouse raise them, don't baby them. They have to race, and they have to be tough."

Nervous owners might flinch from some of his approaches, but raising yearlings in 100-acre fields has yielded excellent results at Stone Farm.

Whether the youngsters are raised in Kentucky or New Zealand, Hancock believes that "you want to maximize their genetic potential, and one way I've tried to do that is to raise them in big fields. If you want to raise a trout, you want to raise it in a big lake versus an aquarium. If you want to raise a good horse, you also need good land and good water that are rich in minerals."

The mineral content of water and the nutrients provided by quality forage are primary considerations that Hancock takes into account as he works with his mares and foals. He said, "My grandfather would get his oats from Michigan, hay from Ohio, getting the best nutrients from different areas."

His point of view in this regard is that you get out what you put in, which he summarized by saying, "Whatever you do, you can't make chicken salad out of chicken shit."

The basic strokes are easy to lay in, and Hancock thinks those are easy, just common sense to people reared working with horses.

The challenge lies in the details, the hundreds of small adjustments and specializations that time, temperament, and even intuition bring to raising top horses. He said, "In each of those things, there's a whole lot of categories which have As, Bs, Cs to them." Those subtle categories make the difference between an acceptable horse and a really pleasing one, the difference between a high-class horse and a champion.

And this is the part of raising Thoroughbreds that is most artful. Hancock said, "Like being a musician or a writer, you learn from those who have done it. You work hard, persevere, listen and learn. I'm 61 years old, and my dad said, 'The older I get, the less I know about this game.' You have to be open to new technology and new ideas. Horses are still the same, but still it's an ongoing education."

Hancock gave an illustration of how much his father knew and how lively their relationship could be. When they were out driving many years ago, Hancock related, "my father told me some things about a farm owned by Mr. King on the right up from Barry Ryan's Normandy Farm. It was real pretty with these white board fences, and I was kind of an agitator and was impressed with those white fences.

"So I said, 'That sure is a pretty farm.'

"He said, 'That farm's never raised a good horse and never will.'

"So I said, 'Now, why couldn't you fertilize that land and raise a good horse?'

"He said, 'No. Never raised a good horse and never will.'

"It's beech-ridge land. That land out there wouldn't raise corn over chest high. The bottoms of this land [here on Stone Farm] will raise corn 12 or 14 feet high. It will produce 3,200 or 3,400 pounds of tobacco to the acre.

"The farms I've bought were ones that I thought had good land. We've raised three Kentucky Derby winners, two seconds (Menifee and Strodes Creek), and a Kentucky Oaks winner. If you don't raise your corn on the right soil, you don't get a good yield. If you don't have a good foundation, I think you're just spinning your wheels.

"Some of the fields on farms I've bought we've had to lime for five years in a row. They've been corned to death, and you have to go in and restore the quality and strength to the soil."

In addition to all the physical elements of land and nutrition, Hancock declares that "You have to have the people, too. If you have everything else, you need the right people to handle the horses. The manager and staff have to be knowledgeable, and you can teach them if they're willing to work and try to learn, even if they don't know that much to begin with.

Arthur feeding Infinidad

"There's an art to being a horseman. I see some people are natural musicians, but others you couldn't teach to play anything. I believe being a horseman is an art and a gift. Some people are good at it. They have a love of animals and a certain type of personality that is happy working outdoors working with animals.

"I think it's a more artistic personality that has an empathy for the animal. But if a person wants to develop that and tries hard, most can do pretty well."

"You got to breed them right. You have to raise them right. You got to get them into good hands, from breaking on through racing. Like Benjamin Franklin said, 'Without the blessing from above, you got no shot to start with,' and I think you might get that blessing by going with the greater force in the universe. If you go with it, do the right thing, treat people well, it should work out for you.

"Keep good karma; don't have a negative attitude. It creates disharmony. I believe that if you have good harmony and good karma, you have more success and more enjoyment."

As a songwriter and singer, horse owner and breeder, son and father, Hancock has found a path for himself, one that lets him be who he is and do what he believes right.

Perhaps because he undertook troubles to find his way, the understanding of right is intensely important to him. He said, "The pendulum swings, and fads come and go. I like the lines in the poem from William Cullen Bryant:

> Truth, crushed to earth, shall rise again;
>
> The eternal years of God are hers;
>
> But Error, wounded, writhes in pain,
>
> And dies among his worshippers.
>
> – from "The Battle-Field"

As someone who has seen the ups and downs of breeding and racing for several decades, Hancock understands the obstacles to success. Yet he chose a path for himself and made it his own. And at Stone Farm, along with friends and associates, he bred two Kentucky Derby winners (Gato del Sol and Fusaichi Pegasus), raised and bought a third (Sunday Silence), and bred and raised a fourth classic winner in Risen Star.

After one of those classic successes, Hancock said, "Raising good horses is what my life's all about, and raising good horses is an art." And a good artist lets his work speak for itself.

# A Champion Returns

Gato Del Sol raced through the age of six for Hancock and Peters, showing competitiveness and toughness while performing well on both dirt and turf. By the time he retired, Gato del Sol had won or placed in 17 stakes events and earned $1,340,107.

However, Arthur Hancock's first Kentucky Derby winner did not turn out to have a successful career at stud. A rangy, long-striding horse who really needed a distance of ground and a fast pace to show his best form, Gato del Sol wasn't the type of stallion prospect who met the immediate desires of the commercial market.

When he retired to stud for the 1986 breeding season, Gato del Sol drew a certain amount of attention. He had evidence of high ability, and his pedigree was an outcross for many lines in the stud book. But he did not appeal to breeders with a goal of breeding quick two-year-olds. And in time, his appeal paled even for those breeders with a dedication for the classics. So Hancock sold Gato del Sol to a farm in Germany with the thought that the stallion might find greater success in siring staying horses on the spacious racecourses of Europe.

That did not happen, as the modest success of Gato del Sol's offspring overseas mirrored his offspring's performances in the U.S. Then, after the horror stories of elderly stallions being sent to slaughterhouses, Arthur and Staci Hancock repurchased the gray son of Cougar for $5,500 and spent more than twice that sum having him shipped home safely.

The arrival of Gato del Sol on an August afternoon in 1999, white with age but bright and happy, was a pleasurable moment for the owners and staff of Stone Farm, who then recalled how he had made them feel 17 years earlier with a victory in the greatest two minutes in sports.

Staff members at Stone Farm welcome Gato del Sol back home.

The Arthur Hancock Family

# CONCLUSION

Looking back at the Hancock family's role in Thoroughbred racing and breeding over the past 50-odd years, it is an understatement to say that the owners of Claiborne farm have been a force in the Thoroughbred world.

Three generations of Hancocks have been contributors to shaping the breed at the highest levels, and their perceptions of bloodstock have had a lasting effect on the Thoroughbred in America and around the world.

At no time, however, have the Hancocks and Claiborne been the only players on the field in the grand game of racing and breeding. The Whitneys, Astors, Rothschilds, Belmonts, and many others have also been contributors at the most exalted level.

Part of what makes the Hancocks stand out is that they have lasted so long and have managed to stay right near the top of the game through a succession of economic and social changes.

With a first-rate operation and world-class stallions, the horse breeders of the Hancock family have managed to combine their understanding of the Thoroughbred with management and consultation for some of the wealthiest and most successful owners and breeders of the past half-century.

Looking into the future, doubtless the same principles will be maintained as both Arthur and Seth Hancock work to perpetuate their visions and successes into the new century and lay foundations for future generations.

Preparing Claiborne or Stone for the future is not as simple now as the task would have been 50 years ago. The world of breeding in

Kentucky has changed radically – much more so in the past 20 years – so that the level of domination that Claiborne maintained for the greater part of the last century realistically may not be possible in the next.

For one thing, not so very long ago the number of major Thoroughbred stallion operations included Claiborne and Spendthrift, with smaller collections of mostly homebred or home-raced stallions at farms like Calumet, Coldstream, Idle Hour, Greentree, and Almahurst.

Today, there are a dozen major stallion operations and a dozen or so more that want to be.

Furthermore, the scale and intensity of the competition among the major operations has increased as the number of stallion owners has multiplied. The size of foal crops has increased, the number of stallions and mares bred has increased, and the competition to attract more and more mares to stallions has increased most of all.

Although this elevation in both the number of elite stallions and the volume of mares chosen to be mated with them seems to contradict the principles of supply and demand, the economics of the stallion market have created this situation.

With more farms standing stallions, the demand for the premium stallion prospects has escalated amazingly over the past few decades. While Secretariat in 1973 made headlines as the most expensive stallion prospect ever with a total syndicated value of slightly more than $6 million, the record figure increased fivefold in a dozen years and tenfold in less than 30 years when Fusaichi Pegasus was purchased in a private transaction as a stallion prospect at a value around $60 million.

Since the competition for premium stallions is driving the Thoroughbred business, every other aspect of farming and planning has to be geared to allow the greatest success in that arena.

Fusaichi Pegasus is a good example of the demands of the new economic structure of breeding. If a stallion prospect with his general value were bred like a stallion in the 1970s, covering 35 to 40 mares annually, it would require a stud fee around $500,000 to recover the cost of the purchase in the course of four years (allowing 30 live foals annually at a fee of a half-million each) with the investors making no profit at all on the investment cost during that time.

What sort of wild man would take a $60 million plunge without the prospect of a profit for several years, if ever?

The savvy international businessman John Magnier took this economic model and stood it on its head. By offering more for the premium stallion prospects that fit his criteria, Magnier stole a march on his competition by purchasing top-end sire prospects and then standing those stallions to much larger books of mares. Instead of 40 mares with 30 or so resulting live foals, the sires at Magnier's Coolmore Stud in Ireland and Ashford in Kentucky began to cover increasingly larger books of mares.

By doubling or tripling the previously accepted number of mares to a stallion, Magnier and his bloodstock commandos were able to do several things at once. First, they could pay more than anyone else to buy the stock they wanted. Then they accelerated their pay-out by making the stud fees reasonably well in line with other stallions but having many more seasons available.

Magnier also added shuttling stallions into the Southern Hemisphere to his economic plan, with the result that whether the stallion succeeds or not, the Coolmore group has made money on the deal before the horse's offspring ever start in a race. And then they go on to the next horse.

Trying to navigate in a turbulent economic stream between the Scylla and Charibdis of the overseas breeding operations that have seemingly bottomless wealth, the Hancocks have chosen to compete on their own terms. Both found the concept of shuttle stallions and mega-books contrary to their way of breeding horses and trying to raise good racehorses.

And one way they have tried to combat the dire competition is to breed horses of their own that are good enough to be stallions. The other is to cultivate clients who will participate in stallions but allow a management of the horse based less on pure economic success.

161

With challenges of this scope in the business of breeding, the future for any horse breeding operation that relies on its own way cannot be called rosy. In time, circumstances may prove out that taking a conservative approach will be the one that carries the day, and the handful of farms that haven't embraced shuttling and vast books of mares may be able to maintain enough quality that quantity cannot overcome them.

With all due respect, however, the future is almost always unforeseeable and potentially dangerous in its unpredictability.

Among the imponderable factors that lie ahead for racing and breeding are the roles that the financing of racing and the nature of the national and the international economies will take in creating or destroying wealth and thus enlarging or constricting the opportunity for many people to be involved with racing.

Who, for instance, in the booming 1920s would have expected a world-wide economic collapse and vast depression? Yet the Great Depression most certainly happened, and it damaged racing and breeding, along with dozens of other endeavors, for a decade or more.

The only very strong probability for the future is that radical changes will happen and that some of them will not be good. These external forces do not mean that Claiborne will cease to exist. Not at all.

The horse breeders of the Hancock family have survived depressions, wars, and changing economies. We now look back and say they prospered and succeeded. But at the time, each man had to make decisions, take chances, and look to the future doing the best he could. And that is still the case today.

We may, in 50 years, look back and say, "What was all that shuttle business about, anyhow?" Or maybe it will have been a watershed in the development of breeding and racing strategies that have greatly prospered at the expense of any others.

The prospects for the years to come are mixed, but by doing their best and staying within the guiding principles and values that help to make racing and breeding a wonderful kind of life, the Hancocks will come out at the end of the day and feel they have done the best for their clients and for themselves.

By sticking to their best principles, each Hancock has faced challenges, suffered losses, found successes, and yet felt he had done the right thing for himself, his friends, and his horses.

In building Stone Farm from an idea into a major breeding farm with an international reputation, Arthur has accomplished all he hoped to do. With classic winners, champions, and leading sires, he carved major successes from disappointments.

In maintaining Claiborne as a leading stallion operation and owner-breeder, Seth has found a path through the briar patch. Along the way he oversaw the breeding of great horses, stood Mr. Prospector and Danzig, and acquired Claiborne's elusive victory in the Kentucky Derby.

The only thing he could not do was to assure that the next supersire was available when the older supersires were gone.

With these accomplishments and many others, the Hancocks, as breeders of the Thoroughbred and upholders of a tradition that places the horse first, have contributed more than dollars and cents to the sport and the breed. They have been part of those who set the tone for how the work is done on farms and how the horse is perceived by the public.

Breeding and raising horses is a humbling business, and the Hancocks have taken their triumphs and their disappointments as parts of the great ride and have carried on.

But by taking a practical and somewhat reserved approach to the fascinating endeavor of breeding a good horse, the Hancock family has helped to build an idea of the way to appreciate the horse and to grow with the journey on the way to breeding a top individual. It is a way of being that emphasizes the joy of the moment and the importance of the day, as well as whatever may come tomorrow.

And all of us, as lovers of the horse and sport, can look out over the fields on a fall evening and take pleasure in the sight. The colored leaves of the tall trees wave in the late breeze, and weanlings in shades of brown mingle with the shadows as they gather at the stream to drink.

The sky is brighter and more colorful than the pastures, as the light tints the clouds with color and highlights. Mares move not quite silently in the broad fields behind us, and we know the wonder of all that is before us and the pleasant expectation of what may come tomorrow.

# Claiborne Stallions

## 1949

Apache (1939 Alcazar x Flying Song, by Sir Gallahad III)
Blenheim (1927 Blandford x Malva, by Charles O'Malley)
Fenelon (1937 Sir Gallahad III x Filante, by Sardanapale)
Fighting Fox (1935 Sir Gallahad III x Marguerite, by Celt)
Gallant Fox (1927 Sir Gallahad III x Marguerite, by Celt)
Hypnotist (1936 Hyperion x Flying Gal, by Sir Gallahad III)
Isolater (1933 Blandford x Priscilla Carter, by Omar Khayyam)
Johnstown (1936 Jamestown x La France, by Sir Gallahad III)
Princequillo (1940 Prince Rose x Cosquillo, by Papyrus)
Rhodes Scholar (1933 Pharos x Book Law, by Buchan)
Sir Gallahad III (1920 Teddy x Plucky Liege, by Spearmint)
Snark (1933 Boojum x Helvetia, by Hourless)
Some Chance (1939 Chance Play x Some Pomp, by Pompey)

## 1950

Ambiorix (1946 Tourbillon x Lavendula, by Pharos)
Bold Irishman  (1938 Sir Gallahad III x Erin, by Transmute)
Black Tarquin (1945 Rhodes Scholar x Vagrancy, by Sir Gallahad III)
Double Jay (1944 Balladier x Broomshot, by Whisk Broom)

## 1951

Nasrullah (1940 Nearco x Mumtaz Begum, by Blenheim)
Prince Simon (1947 Princequillo x Dancing Dora, by Sir Gallahad III)

## 1952

Hill Prince (1947 Princequillo x Hildene, by Bubbling Over)

## 1953

Arise (1946 He Did x Coralie B., by Apprehension)

## 1954

Dark Star (1950 Royal Gem x Isolde, by Bull Dog)

**1955**

To Market (1948 Market Wise x Pretty Does, by Johnstown)
Turn-to (1951 Royal Charger x Source Sucree, by Admiral Drake)

**1956**

**1957**

Flying Fury (1952 Nasrullah x Sicily, by Reaping Reward)
Nantallah (1953 Nasrullah x Shimmer, by Flares)
Tulyar (1949 Tehran x Neocracy, by Nearco)

**1958**

Dedicate (1952 Princequillo x Dini, by John P. Grier)
Nance's Lad (1952 Slide Rule x Nance's Ace, by Case Ace)

**1959**

Bold Ruler (1954 Nasrullah x Miss Disco, by Discovery)
Court Martial (1942 Fair Trial x Instantaneous, by Hurry On)

**1960**

Nadir (1955 Nasrullah x Gallita, by Challenger)
Round Table (1954 Princequillo x Knight's Daughter, by Sir Cosmo)

**1961**

Bagdad (1956 Double Jay x Bazura, by Blue Peter)
Dunce (1956 Tom Fool x Ghazni, by Mahmoud)
Hillsdale (1955 Take Away x Johann, by Johnstown)
Top Charger (1956 Royal Charger x Popularity, by Alibhai)

**1962**

Middle Brother (1956 Hill Prince x Alablue, by Blue Larkspur)
Whodunit (1955 Princequillo x Who Dini, by Hypnotist)

**1963**

Ridan (1959 Nantallah x Rough Shod, by Gold Bridge)
Sir Gaylord (1959 Turn-to x Somethingroyal, by Princequillo)

**1964**

Hitting Away (1958 Ambiorix x Striking, by War Admiral)

**1965**

Herbager (1956 Vandale x Flagette, by Escamillo)
Pago Pago (1960 Matrice x Pompilia, by Abbots Fell)
Tatan (1952 The Yuvaraj x Valkyrie, by Donatello)

**1966**

Decidedly (1959 Determine x Gloire Fille, by War Glory)
Hurry to Market (1961 To Market x Hasty Girl, by Princequillo)
Jacinto (1962 Bold Ruler x Cascade, by Precipitation)

**1967**

Bold Lad (1962 Bold Ruler x Misty Morn, by Princequillo)
Hill Rise (1961 Hillary x Red Curtain, by Russia)
Sky High (1957 Star Kingdom x Flight's Daughter, by Helios)
Tom Rolfe (1962 Ribot x Pocahontas, by Roman)

**1968**

Buckpasser (1963 Tom Fool x Busanda, by War Admiral)
Forli (1963 Aristophanes x Trevisa, by Advocate)

**1969**

Damascus (1964 Sword Dancer x Kerala, by My Babu)
Pretense (1963 Endeavour x Imitation, by Hyperion)

**1970**

Drone (1966 Sir Gaylord x Cap and Bells, by Tom Fool)
Hawaii (1964 Utrillo x Ethane, by Mehrali)
Pronto (1958 Timor x Prosperino, by Gusty)

**1971**

Cabildo (1963 Round Table x Delta, by Nasrullah)
Nijinsky (1967 Northern Dancer x Flaming Page, by Bull Page)
Reviewer (1966 Bold Ruler x Broadway, by Hasty Road)
Sir Ivor (1965 Sir Gaylord x Attica, by Mr. Trouble)
Tell (1966 Round Table x Nas-Mahal, by Nasrullah)

**1972**

Ack Ack (1966 Battle Joined x Fast Turn, by Turn-to)
Fiddle Isle (1965 Bagdad x Nascania, by Nasrullah)
Hoist the Flag (1968 Tom Rolfe x Wavy Navy, by War Admiral)
Le Fabuleux (1961 Wild Risk x Anguar, by Verso)
Sir Wiggle (1965 Sadair x Wiggle, by Rego)

**1973**

Bold Reasoning (1968 Boldnesian x Reason to Earn,
   by Hail to Reason)
Restless Wind (1956 Windy City x Lump Sugar, by Bull Lea)

**1974**

Bold Reason (1968 Hail to Reason x Lalun, by Djeddah)
Riva Ridge (1969 First Landing x Iberia, by Heliopolis)
Secretariat (1970 Bold Ruler x Somethingroyal, by Princequillo)

**1975**

Judger (1971 Damascus x Face the Facts, by Court Martial)

**1976**

**1977**

Avatar (1972 Graustark x Brown Berry, by Mount Marcy)
Navajo (1970 Grey Dawn x Doublene, by Double Jay)

**1978**

Honest Pleasure (1973 What a Pleasure x Tularia, by Tulyar)
Majestic Light (1973 Majestic Prince x Irradiate, by Ribot)

**1979**

Believe It (1975 In Reality x Breakfast Bell, by Buckpasser)
Buckfinder (1974 Buckpasser x Shenanigans, by Native Dancer)

**1980**

Coastal (1976 Majestic Prince x Alluvial, by Buckpasser)
Cox's Ridge (1974 Best Turn x Our Martha, by Ballydonnell)
Topsider (1974 Northern Dancer x Drumtop, by Round Table)

**1981**
Danzig (1977 Northern Dancer x Pas de Nom, by Admiral's Voyage)
It's True (1976 In Reality x Breakfast Bell, by Buckpasser)
Mr. Prospector (1970 Raise a Native x Gold Digger, by Nashua)
Private Account (1976 Damascus x Numbered Account,
  by Buckpasser)
Spectacular Bid (1976 Bold Bidder x Spectacular, by Promised Land)

**1982**
Key to Content (1977 Forli x Key Bridge, by Princequillo)
Quadratic (1975 Quadrangle x Smartaire, by Quibu)

**1983**
Conquistador Cielo (1979 Mr. Prospector x K D Princess,
  by Bold Commander)

**1984**
Devil's Bag (1981 Halo x Ballade, by Herbager)
Linkage (1979 Hoist the Flag x Unity Hall, by Cyane)

**1985**
Go Step (1975 Bold Reasoning x Miss Quickstep, by Native Dancer)

**1986**
Track Barron (1981 Buckfinder x Golden Spike, by Sir Gaylord)
Vanlandingham (1981 Cox's Ridge x Populi, by Star Envoy)

**1987**
none

**1988**
Ogygian (1983 Damascus x Gonfalon, by Francis S.)
Polish Navy (1984 Danzig x Navsup, by Tatan)

## 1989

Demons Begone (1984 Elocutionist x Rowdy Angel, by Halo)
Ferdinand (1983 Nijinsky x Banja Luka, by Double Jay)
Forty Niner (1985 Mr. Prospector x File, by Tom Rolfe)

## 1990

Proper Reality (1985 In Reality x Proper Princess, by Nodouble)
Seeking the Gold (1985 Mr. Prospector x Con Game,
   by Buckpasser)

## 1991

Easy Goer (1986 Alydar x Relaxing, by Buckpasser)

## 1992

Academy Award (1986 Secretariat x Mine Only, by Mr. Prospector)
Talinum (1984 Alydar x Water Lily, by Riverman)

## 1993

## 1994

Sultry Song (1988 Cox's Ridge x Sultry Sun, by Buckfinder)

## 1995

Boundary (1990 Danzig x Edge, by Damascus)
Lure (1989 Danzig x Endear, by Alydar)
Take Me Out (1988 Cure the Blues x White Feather, by Tom Rolfe)

## 1996

Go for Gin (1991 Cormorant x Never Knock, by Stage Door Johnny)
Private Terms (1985 Private Account x Laughter, by Bold Ruler)

## 1997

Our Emblem (1991 Mr. Prospector x Personal Ensign,
   by Private Account)
Unbridled (1987 Fappiano x Gana Facil, by Le Fabuleux)

**1998**

Benny the Dip (1994 Silver Hawk x Rascal Rascal, by Ack Ack)

Pulpit (1994 A.P. Indy x Preach, by Mr. Prospector)

**1999**

Arch (1995 Kris S. x Aurora, by Danzig)

Coronado's Quest (1995 Forty Niner x Laughing Look, by Damascus)

Ordway (1994 Salt Lake x Priceless Countess, by Vaguely Noble)

**2000**

Horse Chestnut (1995 Fort Wood x London Wall, by Col. Pickering)

Out of Place (1987 Cox's Ridge x Arabian Dancer, by Damascus)

**2001**

**2002**

Monarchos (1998 Maria's Mon x Regal Band, by Dixieland Band)

**2003**

**2004**

Flatter (1999 A.P. Indy x Praise, by Mr. Prospector)

**2005**

During (2000 Cherokee Run x Blading Saddle, by Blade)

Stroll (2000 Pulpit x Maid for Walking, by Prince Sabo)

Strong Hope (2000 Grand Slam x Shining Through,
   by Deputy Minister)